Old Missouri barns are a lot like people -- each one has a story to tell. Some were built during the earliest settlement periods, many survived the Civil War years, while others have stood standing through blizzards, tornados, and floods. Some of Missouri's barns have been well cared for, and many historic barns have been saved by owners, clubs, and civic organizations. Other barns have been needlessly lost, due to neglect, abandonment, and the forces of change and development. We need to preserve these monuments to our past. *Rural Missouri* hopes to help do that with sponsorship of this book.

Barns of Missouri: Storehouses of History, written by an authority on the subject, Dr. Howard Marshall of the University of Missouri-Columbia, takes us on a tour through Missouri to visit some of our many interesting and historic barns. Going beyond pictures, this book tells us where our barn concepts come from, and how and why barns vary from region to region and community to community. Best of all, this book preserves, through written and visual documentation, important features of traditional architecture that contribute so much to our daily lives and to future generations.

MoDOT
Photos
1. Round barn
(Adair Co.)
2. William Gentry
Barn

RURAL
M I S S O U R I
The voice of Missouri's electric cooperatives

Missouri's Electric Cooperatives

For additional book copies contact:

Rural Missouri
P.O. Box 1645
Jefferson City, MO 65109

Phone: (573) 659-3423
Fax: (573) 636-9499
www.ruralmissouri.org

Missouri's rural electric cooperatives and their official publication *Rural Missouri* are proud to present Barns of Missouri: Storehouse of History. Through exhaustive research, field work, photography and personal recollections, author Howard Marshall and the *Rural Missouri* staff have preserved forever the beauty and history of these endangered structures that add so much to the landscape of our great state.

When electricity first came to the countryside, it was Missouri's electric cooperatives that lit the barns when others said the job could not be done. By providing power to farmers, electric cooperatives raised the standard of living for rural people. Electricity became a new hired hand that made American farmers the most productive in the world.

Just as old barns have found new roles on the family farm, electric cooperatives over the years have gone beyond merely providing electricity to their members. They have labored to ensure rural people are no longer second-class citizens by bringing jobs, essential services and a new concern for community to the countryside.

Barns have always been a symbol of the value of hard work. For this reason we are proud to be associated with this project.

(Below) Randolph County, formerly on Highway 63, south of Jacksonville. (Photo by Pat B. Clark)

Chariton County, west of Bynumville. (Photo by Pat B. Clark)

BARNS OF MISSOURI
STOREHOUSES OF HISTORY

by

Howard Wight Marshall

Professor Emeritus of Art History and Archaeology
University of Missouri–Columbia

THE
DONNING COMPANY
PUBLISHERS

DEDICATION

For Butch, Pete, Minnie, Jennings, Tippy,
and Bonnie, farm dogs.

The Donning Company Publishers
184 Business Park Drive, Suite 206
Virginia Beach, VA 23462

Ed Williams, Project Directors
Steve Mull, General Manager
Barbara B. Buchanan, Office Manager
Richard A. Horwege, Senior Editor
Thad Pickett, Graphic Designer
Scott Rule, Imaging Artist
Mary Ellen Wheeler, Proofreader/Editorial Assistant
Lori D. Kennedy, Project Research Coordinator
Scott Rule, Director of Marketing
Travis Gallup, Marketing Coordinator

Library of Congress Cataloging-in-Publication Data

Marshall, Howard W.
        Barns of Missouri : storehouses of history / by Howard
Wight Marshall.
        p. cm.
    Includes bibliographical references and index.
    ISBN 1-57864-231-0 (hardcover : alk. paper)
    1. Barns—Missouri. I. Title.

NA8230.M353 2003
728'.922'09778—dc22

                                        2003063495

Printed in the United States of America

(Right) Timber and red brick barn, Linn County.
(photo by Thad Pickett)
(Cover) Livingston County, south of Chillicothe.
(photo by Scott Rule)

CONTENTS

Round barn in Adair County. (Pat B. Clark)

FOREWORD

OFFICE OF THE SECRETARY OF STATE
STATE OF MISSOURI
JEFFERSON CITY
65101

STATE CAPITOL
ROOM 208
(573) 751-2379

MATT BLUNT
SECRETARY OF STATE

October 2, 2003

Dear Friends:

I am pleased to offer these words in support of Professor Howard Marshall's long-awaited book <u>Barns of Missouri: Storehouses of History</u>, a well-researched yet accessible study celebrating our common past. This beautifully illustrated book will be welcome among classroom teachers, students, and scholars, as well as general readers interested in discovering – or rediscovering – the story of rural Missouri.

This book also serves the timely function of cultural conservation. We know all too well that our legacy of barns and agricultural buildings, which once were familiar to all Missourians, are lost everyday to the forces of nature and of change. Dr. Marshall's <u>Barns of Missouri</u> provides a handy documentary guide to future generations who may one day wonder where so many of the old barns went.

It gives me special pleasure that the Missouri State Archives, a division of my office, could be part of this important project. A number of historic photographs were drawn from our collections, and many more are available than the few that could be published in the present book.

Finally, I wish to recognize the fine work produced by Jim McCarty and his staff at *Rural Missouri Magazine*, the monthly publication of the Associated Electric Cooperatives of Missouri. We are lucky to have these dedicated Missourians publishing accounts that tell the stories of not only the rural electric industry but many other facets of Missouri's cultural heritage.

Sincerely,

Matt Blunt

Matt Blunt

PREFACE

Indeed everything in our present landscape tells us something about the past if only we can learn how to interpret it.

—W. G. Hoskins

Old barns have been a focus of my work as a researcher, teacher, and writer for many years. Writing this book, I was given a chance to sit down and write a well-illustrated general overview of the history of barns in Missouri.

How could one book cover barns throughout such a complex and diverse state? I proceeded with the hope of presenting a basic introduction, perhaps a preliminary survey or primer, and not a full scholarly treatise. Readers may find their personal favorites missing, but I hope I have produced a useful introductory historical and architectural survey of this rich subject.

This book therefore proceeds from an effort to combine a sense of historical time with a presentation of the major barn *types* in our state. Those types are the *single-crib barn* (the basic building block, built in every community), the so-called *English barn* (from the British Isles and Europe) and its siblings the hewn-log *double-crib barn* (built throughout Missouri by early settlers no matter what their backgrounds) and the *bank barn* (often preferred by German-speaking farmers). The final type is the *transverse-crib barn*, a prevalent form with origins in the nineteenth century upper Southern United States.

Along with those major barn types, we will look at some round and octagonal barns, a rather odd class of structures that had its heyday around the turn of the twentieth century. We will take a moment to look at modern pole barns, the prefabricated buildings using new technologies that have all but replaced the old-time carpenter. We also will look at some "barn like" structures that are familiar ingredients in the rural landscape, such as mills and covered bridges.

My friends at *Rural Missouri* and Donning Publishing made it clear our book would be useful to researchers and students, but it also should be inviting to "general audiences." There are some notes and discussion which I hope will be of assistance to teachers, students, planners, historians, preservationists, and others concerned about how and why we need to document, conserve, and reuse Missouri's vacant or decaying barns for future generations. The picture of Missouri history can only be complete when textbook writers and teachers begin to include the everyday sheds and stables along with buildings connected to famous architects and successful citizens.

I have been photographing old barns for something like forty years. But most of my research has been located in three regions: The counties in Little Dixie (generally north of

Billy Lee's memories of his birthplace, the William Axford Lee farm southeast of Wright City in Warren County, are rendered vividly in his 2002 relief carving on a two-inch pine board depicting the farm in 1929. (Courtesy Billy Lee)

Locust Grove Farm, built in the 1830s in the Milton community of Randolph County by my great-great-grandfather, typifies the Little Dixie traditions in architecture and farm layout—a timber framed two-story I-house type with a transverse-crib barn type—as well as the omnipresent draft mules. The new house (1938), where I spent my first years, was designed by my mother, Frances Jennings Marshall, a descendent of the original builders and owners who came from Bluegrass Kentucky in mover wagons. (Unknown photographer circa 1950)

the Missouri River and east of the Mississippi for a certain distance); portions of the French-American Old Mines community in the eastern Ozarks; and portions of the "Rhineland" of German-speaking settlement.

In working on this book, therefore, I engaged a number of friends and compatriots to help. Certain regions of the state will be better represented than others. Yet, travelers know that some parts of Missouri are thick with old barns while in other regions barns are scarce. Those facts are sharply reflected in the settlement and economic history, and indeed the environmental history, of our state and its people.

Many people think the barns scattered across the landscape are nothing more than relics or simple shelters for crops and livestock. Some see old barns as charming bits of nostalgia reminiscent of "The Good Old Days". Some see them as scruffy eyesores. Rural fire departments often consider decrepit barns as good places to practice starting and putting out fires. The traditional hay and livestock barn is an endangered species.

In the introduction to one of the memorable 1880s Missouri county histories, the anonymous writer offers this:

The lapse of time, the advance of civilization, the wonderful scientific discoveries that within the past 40 years have added so much to the comfort and pleasure of the world, have had the effect to make life so roseate with the hue of an easy-going and tranquil existence that the privations, hardships and dangers of the pioneer settlers are overlooked, undervalued and forgotten. (History of St. Charles, Montgomery, and Warren Counties, Missouri)

I trust that present and future Missourians will continue to find ways to deny the bitterness in such statements. People learn about history from their environments, books, depictions in the media, and stories told around the supper table. A major element in our feelings about history is the buildings we see and know. We learn about our past by experiencing architecture. Buildings shape our ideas about who we are and where we come from. For a more complete picture of our Missouri past, we need barns. The house and barn of the pioneer are more than just shelter, they are statements of family history, ambition, economy.

Barns are essential in the workaday world, yet the kinds of old barns we treasure are rapidly being erased by the intractable currents of change. Perhaps through this book, we may come to better know the wealth of barns in Missouri. Perhaps we may begin to challenge ourselves, beyond nostalgia, to find new ways to appreciate these old structures and find ways to conserve this great legacy for the benefit of future generations.

ACKNOWLEDGMENTS

I have been helped by a number of people in preparing this book. I thank Steve Mull, whose enthusiasm and guidance helped enormously, as well as Scott Rule, Thad Pickett and others at Donning for their help.

I also was reminded of Jim McCarty's journalist's guideline—"You don't use 'first,' 'last,' and 'only'" in writing about your subject. I appreciated working with Jim McCarty and Jeff Joiner at *Rural Missouri*, old friends with deep knowledge of Missouri. Their devotion to understanding and documenting our heritage of traditional life and work is splendid.

Most of the photos came from my old Canon 35mm cameras and slide film. A few images were in Kodacolor with a point-and-shoot camera. Those images were made between the late 1960s and 2003, and many of the earlier photos were part of my dissertation research at Indiana University on old buildings in Little Dixie. A number of photos were provided by others, and they are identified in captions. In the captions, if no photographer is give, the photograph was taken by the author. Additional photographs courtesy of Michael Broggie, David L. Burton (Springfield), Pat Clark (Brookfield), Mary Daniel (Stoutsville), Travis W. Gallup (Marceline), Brian Genovese (Bolivar), Billy Lee (Wright City), Ed McKinney (West Plains), Margot Ford McMillen (Millersburg), John D. Marshall (Minneapolis, MN), Ryan Mooney (Springfield), Lynn Morrow (Jefferson City), Osmund Overby (Columbia), Thad Pickett (Marceline) and Scott Rule (Marceline). We found helpful images by Jim McCarty, Bob McEowen, and Jeff Joiner in the archives of *Rural Missouri*.

In Missouri we have excellent archives and historical collections, and these have been helpful for historic photographs. Thanks are due to Dr. Toni Prawl, Sue Olson, and Robert J. Reeder in the Cultural Resources office of the Missouri Department of Transportation in Jefferson City; Laura R. Jolley at the Missouri State Archives in Jefferson City, and Lee Gilleard, Roger Maserang, and Alison Dubbert of the State Historic Preservation Program in the Department of Natural Resources. Not only are these agencies important in conserving our shared cultural heritage, their staffs are helpful and professional. Most of all I thank my longtime teacher, friend, and colleague at the University of Missouri, Osmund Overby, for his continued guidance; and my wife, Margot Ford McMillen, for reading parts of the manuscript and making suggestions.

Among the many others to thank are Harvie Atterbury (Fulton), Lewis Baumgartner (Millersburg), Aubrey M. Bradley Jr. (Huntsville), Ray Brassieur (Lafayette, LA), Cliff Bryan (West Plains), Tom Carneal (Maryville), Bill Crawford (Columbia), Patrick Dougherty (Columbia), Susan Flader (Columbia), Lynn Gentzler (Columbia), Carl Herd (Wright City), J. R. Hickam (Jamestown), Patricia and Bill Holmes (Boonville), Billy and Betty Lee (Wright City), Joseph Lindell (St. Louis), Knox and Nelda McCrory (Columbia), Jim and Karen Marschel (Warrenton), John D. Marshall (Minneapolis, MN), Ed McKinney (West Plains), Marjorie Miller (Montgomery City), Billie Mills (Perryville), Paul Pepper (Columbia), Toni Prawl (Jefferson City), Hershel Price (Jackson), Alex Riddles (Columbia), Dorothy Ann Bradley Robb and Lemuel Robb (Huntsville), Dolf and Becky Schroeder (Columbia), Walter Schroeder (Columbia), Ken Schneeberger (Columbia), Sally Sprague (Jefferson City), Ray and Mary Theresa Thebeau (Cadet), Deborah Slade Thompson (Columbia), Llona Weiss (Jefferson City), Bob Wilcox (Moberly), staff at the Daniel Boone Home in Defiance (Pam Jensen, Cathy Schoppenhorst, and Greta Maxheimer) and at Faust Park in Chesterfield (Jesse Francis, Wayne Gronefeld, and Jack Hanewinkel).

Those I wish to thank the most are those gone from us, the families and builders of former times whose old barns we pause to study and contemplate. Their spirits endure in the land, and the land remembers.

Howard Wight Marshall
Fulton, Missouri

In Monroe County near the North Fork of the historic Salt River, 1974.

To understand people, understand their buildings. To build for the future, study the past. Learn to value your legacy as you embrace change.

CONSIDERING BARNS

Barn dances with fiddle music and square dance callers are held here. (Photo by Jeff Joiner 2002)

(Left) The Young family barn, a transverse-crib type most common among pioneers from Kentucky, Tennessee, and other parts of the upper South. Built circa 1920. (Courtesy of Steve and Debbie Young)

A fine example of a three-bay threshing barn (variously called a double-crib, English, or Yankee barn), resembling in form and use (if not in construction) countless barns in Britain and German-speaking Europe; the house, too, is based on British antecedents. (Adair County 1990)

Americans use the word *barn* many ways, befitting its ancient purposes, flexible personality, and its omnipresence across the landscape. In Great Britain, however, the meaning of barn has always been rather narrow. There, the word *barn* simply means, "A covered building for storage of grain; and, in wider usages of hay, straw, flax, and other produce of the earth."[1] Other buildings with different functions were traditional in Europe, with "stables" for horses and oxen, "pig sties" for hogs, and "byres" for the milk cows.

The main type of British and European threshing barn is a fairly simple rectangular structure where the harvested cereals and grains were threshed by hand, using flails. The grain was laid out on the threshing floor, and people swung the flails down to beat the grains loose from the stalk and straw. The grain could then be "winnowed" (or tossed into the air) from large fans or trays, so that the wheat grains became separated from the "chaff." Two big doors facing each other were oriented to the prevailing winds, with the result that the wind itself was a vital tool in flailing and winnowing grains. The straw left over from the process became feed and bedding for livestock. Extra straw and threshed grain, and various pieces of farm equipment, could be stored in the two bays that flanked the threshing floor at the ends of the barn.[2]

Their hand-threshing implements had been used across the British Isles, Scandinavia, and Europe—that marvelous ancient tool called the *flail*. Made in many shapes and sizes, flails share a basic function that guides their design: workers swung their flails down upon the grain so that the seeds were knocked loose. The threshed grains were then "winnowed" using a variety of large woven baskets or fans that allowed the lighter chaff to be lifted off and the heavier grains settling in the basket or pan. Other grains, as they shook loose from the chaff and straw, filtered down upon a broad canvas or a well-sealed and cleaned stone or wooden floor. Leftover straw was collected and used as animal fodder, bedding, and for other purposes on the farm.

Relatively few of the older threshing barns are left. On the "Garbithill" farmstead in the Scottish Lowlands on the edge of the moors, an old stone threshing barn remains, in need of a new roof. The barn at Garbithill is the kind where hand-threshing with flails and *sheeling* (winnowing) were done on the floor in an open bay. The open bay here, as in all other barns where handwork was done, is situated carefully with the roof aligned north to south so that the prevailing winds from the west and southwest could rush through. The two doors, placed exactly opposite, were opened at angles to catch the wind and assist the threshers and winnowers in their dusty work.

The persistence of this ancient rectangular barn shape, with the big doors facing each other, is good evidence of the strength of older traditions in Missouri. There was little need for the two large opposing doors after the Industrial Revolution had brought threshing machines to the farm. But the big doors continued to be made and used, if not for threshing then for bringing in more fresh air and light and to admit larger vehicles and machinery. And while relatively few of these old British threshing barns were built in Missouri stone, countless barns were erected here in wood, the great Missouri building material.

The stable (for horses) and byre (for cattle) in older traditions in Europe and Britain were attached to the dwelling itself. Numerous examples across the United Kingdom remain in use, for this is a very practical way to build a farmstead. In the United States, the various functional parts—stable, dairy, barn, cart shed, etc.—were broken apart and given separate spaces on the larger pieces of landscape available here.

Barns and stables frequently appear in early literature and in the Bible (e.g., Luke 12:24), in the writings of Chaucer, Shakespeare, and countless others. The word is a good example of the process in which old words change their meanings. The word we use today comes from the Old English *byre-ern*—"barley place." In Saxon times, barley was a principal cereal crop harvested

Livestock and grain farm on the windswept Yorkshire moors in northeastern England; the stone house is, in its shape, virtually identical to countless Missouri farmhouses. (1988)

in England, and it required a large, dry storage shelter. The word then gradually changed to *bern* in Middle English and thence to the modern word *barn*.[3]

Only the earliest generations of Missouri farmers needed to cut, gather, thresh, and winnow by hand. By the 1840s, various kinds of newly developed mechanical reapers and binders (drawn by horses, mules, and oxen) could sweep through fields in record time. Just as gasoline- and diesel-powered tractors replaced most of the mules, horses, and oxen (except in special circumstances such as logging and in special communities such as the Amish), mechanical threshing machines all but eliminated the old-fashioned flail and winnowing basket.

The eighteenth and nineteenth centuries were the formative period for the bulk of Missouri's European-based architectural heritage. Just as during the colonial period in the East, many of the first buildings on the new landscapes were farm dwellings and associated structures.

In the glory days of Missouri agriculture, boosters such as the famous journalist and historian Walter Williams wrote:

Eighteenth-century sheep farm in northwestern England in the mountainous Lake District; the fine stone dwelling resembles again the prevailing large two-story Missouri farmhouse of the nineteenth century; the jumble of attached barns includes a threshing barn (partially hidden). (1988)

In Northern Ireland (source of countless Missouri "Scotch Irish" pioneers), a "house and byre" that also has side-by-side spaces for the family and the animals; the front gives little indication that around back there is a door for the stable (for the family's milk cows) on the end of the stone building. (1988)

The distinctive regions that make up Missouri reflect patterns of settlement, spoken dialect, and other features of cultural heritage, and they reflect the nuances of geology and geography. These factors and others gradually gave us a state of vaguely bordered but distinctive cultural and even architectural regions. (WPA Guide to 1930s Missouri)

Within 250 miles of the capital of Missouri, in 1900, were: First, the center of the total farm acreage of the United States; second, the center of corn production; third, the center of farm value; fourth, the center of the improved farm acreage; fifth, the center of the production of the six leading cereals; sixth, the center of the gross income from farms; seventh, the center of oat production; also within the center, but not on the map, was the center of wheat production. In 1904 the center of each was nearer the capital of Missouri and all, with possibly two exceptions, are now within the limits of this State.[4]

Native Americans who had lived here for thousands of years left few permanent structures. Native Americans in the southeastern United States built wooden granaries on poles, but none seem to have been built in our region. For storage, Indian peoples used *caches* (a French term), as did the European-American hunters, trappers, and pioneers. The *cache* was a deep bell-shaped pit, bell-shaped mound, or sheltered space where surplus food, supplies, and possessions could be hidden and protected.

Perhaps the most famous storage structure associated with the prehistoric people in Missouri is Graham Cave, a natural rock shelter in Montgomery County (an excellent State Park open to the public) that was used as long ago as ten thousand years. Archaeologists such as the great Carl Chapman found that other caves were used for storage, but no built storage structures have survived intact.[5]

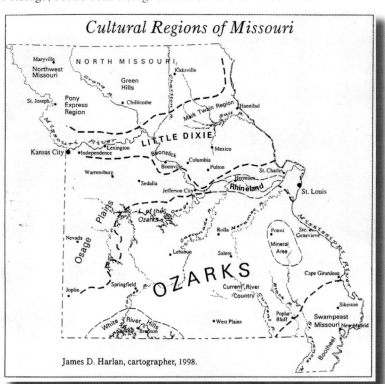

Cultural Regions of Missouri

James D. Harlan, cartographer, 1998.

Because essentially they were hunters, gatherers, and subsistence and seasonal agriculturalists, in earliest times there was little surplus harvest to require the development of barn-like constructions.[6]

It is probable that food and crops were stored in conjunction with the "mounds, ditches, and embankments" and other earthworks, such as the familiar burial mounds (sometimes covered with logs and earth), that were part of ceremonial structures of later times, and it is probable that corn (maize) was stored for the seasonal corn rituals.[7]

Pit-type storage structures were also used during later prehistoric times when Indian peoples began to live in organized towns. Some of these towns were large, such as the Cahokia–St. Louis metropolis on both sides of the Mississippi River. Cahokia, with some fifty thousand population at its peak, was the largest city in North America (circa A.D. 900–1700). This was an important trade and manufacturing center for peoples up and down the Mississippi and lower Missouri Valleys. Chapman writes that their dwellings (which could be thought of as variations on the familiar wigwam structure of the Eastern woodlands) were "square, wooden, or round and had wooden frameworks and thatched roofs" and Nabakov and Easton show that there are tantalizing indications that houses of round logs were built at Cahokia at the time of European contact.[8] At the time of contact with the French in the 1720s, archaeologists have shown that Missouri and Osage Indians were building bell-shaped storage pits in central Missouri, as separate structures or inside lodges.[9] The city completely disappeared within a generation of European contact in the 1700s.

Many Missourians identify themselves as having Native American ethnicity. Some are descendents of Osage and Missouri Native peoples whose tribes were relocated by forced removal westward according to government policies in the territorial and early statehood times, culminating with the 1839 Indian Removal Act. Many more Missourians are descendents of Indians from the Southeast who were forced to leave their homelands on the infamous 1838–1839 "Trail of Tears." This event forced thousands of Cherokees to trek across the Ozarks, roughly from Cape Girardeau across through Springfield, to make new homes on government lands in the Oklahoma Territory.[10]

A great number of Cherokee people stayed here. They married into European-American and African-American communities, and were assimilated to some degree. Many Cherokee had English names and were already farmers or familiar with European-American agricultural systems in the 1830s back in Tennessee or North Carolina. Indian farmers built barns on their farms, and it is hoped that future research may document their barns and other buildings in Missouri. It is probable that their barns were much like those of their European-American neighbors. Studies in the Eastern United States suggest this is so.

Missouri developed as a colonial territory by turns owned by the French and Spanish in the seventeenth and eighteenth centuries and then by the fledgling United States after a famous 1803 land deal of President Thomas Jefferson's called the Louisiana Purchase. The territory became a state in 1821 and was quickly settled

Historic illustrations offer much in our study of Missouri architecture. Several barns and small outbuildings peak our curiosity in this 1859 sketch of the City of Jefferson. (Courtesy Dottie Dallmeyer, in her wonderful *Jefferson City, Missouri* 2000)

by British-American frontiersmen, farmers, and business people. With its gateway character in St. Louis and along its two major rivers dividing "east" from "west," Missouri was both a meeting place and a "jumping off place" for settlers, immigrants, and people heading further west.

Three broad groups of settlers and immigrants played essential roles in the evolution of today's historic cultural landscape and in the construction of the wealth of important buildings in our state. The first group was the French, beginning in the 1700s in places like Ste. Genevieve (the first permanent settlement in Missouri) and St. Louis.

Next were the Anglo-Americans (often called "old stock Americans"), most of them of British ancestry who came from Virginia, Kentucky, and other upland South states beginning around 1790 and growing dominant politically and economically after the Louisiana Purchase. Next came the German-speaking Missourians, a large and prominent group making an enormous impact in the 1830s and 1840s. As census reports and academic studies show, most Missourians today identify their ethnic heritage as based in the British Isles or German-speaking Europe.

Other important groups have left their mark on Missouri's landscape, including African-Americans, largely through their rarely documented role as slaves building structures on farms before Emancipation. While other groups are quite important in the state's history—the Native Americans, Italians, Hispanics—these groups had rather less imprint on the cultural landscape of agriculture and farm buildings.

Like any state, Missouri is made up of definable regions that can be mapped out in a variety of ways. The Department of Natural Resources map divides Missouri into regions based on geography and where the major rivers run. Our state highway map gives us the highways and roads and is also based on a desire to understand the state as a place of plains, prairies, hills, valleys, and rivers. One helpful map in understanding settlement history—and why certain kinds of barns are found in north Missouri and not in the Ozarks (for example)—outlines vernacular regions. Also based on physical setting and geography, it shows different folk regions and local names people give to their own regions, a helpful tool in thinking about local history.

Traditional buildings have discernible connections to the geography and geology of any given area, since especially in earlier times the builders were to some degree dependent upon the locally available construction materials and supplies they could find or acquire nearby.

Interest in old barns has been advanced by increasing attention to local and regional history. The historic preservation movement, creative work by state agencies such as the Missouri Department of Transportation, Missouri Department of Natural Resources, and "living history" museums, have saved and brought attention to a number of barns that would have gone under the wrecking ball.

Patterns of Custom and Memory

The farmer's barn is one of the most memorable elements in the constellation of structures and landscapes we call vernacular architecture. Vernacular—also called traditional, or folk—buildings are erected using time-honored methods, usually learned through apprenticeship and shared experience, and usually without direction from professional academically trained architects or institutional classes.[1] The goal of this kind of design and construction is to make buildings that fit with prevailing and accepted traditions in the community, instead of structures coming from current fashions.

Like other features of tradition, the vernacular building process is founded on inherited ideas and skills that persist in the midst of changes and models from outside the community or region. Traditional building combines sensible old habits with the kind of variations and innovations that meet the community's expectations, needs, and ideals. Design values are deep within the local community's traditional ways of doing things.

Many barns are hand-built by their owners and other barns are built by crews that travel from one neighborhood to another. One interesting feature of traditional building is the close degree to which the client, family, and members of the community participate. The barn builder's ideas and proposals are tuned to the needs of the farm family. This sometimes means there is less room for pure creativity than in high-style design of architects, but that is taken for granted. People apply decorative details and variations to give their barn special character. Even a "simple" barn turns out to exhibit ornamental details and "style."

Most buildings, whether in rural towns or along a county road, can be included in a broad definition of *vernacular architecture*, since few structures were designed by professional architects. There are exceptions, of course, such as the occasional round or octagonal barn. In any community, we may find lots of variation in elements such as barn colors as well as forms and construction methods.

Typical barns? There is variety even within one county, Boone. The use of similar colors as well as barn forms (types) helps give barns regional identity, but diversity and personal choice are always present.

(Top Left) Frame transverse-crib barn with a gambrel roof (offering more space in the hay loft). (1974)

(Below) A double-crib or English barn, unpainted, with main doors on the long side rather than in the gable ends. (1975)

(Bottom Left) A transverse-crib barn, left to weather naturally with no applied paint, with shed additions to offer more space for feeding and sheltering livestock. (1974)

Form

In order for the pattern to be efficiently repeated as farmers clear ground and stake out a barn, it has to be deeply ingrained as to what a "barn" or "house" is and looks like. These structure patterns—what scholars call *types*—developed centuries ago, often in the old countries across the Atlantic. At some point around fifteen hundred years ago the Missouri barn's ancestors were born in northwestern Europe—chiefly among people in the British Isles and among German-speaking peoples of western Europe. Even today, farmers continue to build barns by the time-honored geometry set in motion long ago.

The basic building block of traditional Missouri barn (and house) types is a square or rectangle.[2] For that basic building block, or single-crib barn, to be successfully repeated and desirable, it has to answer the basic needs of its functional goals. So, a one-crib horse barn has to be a certain size, perhaps no smaller than twelve by twelve feet, in order to provide one stall to stable a horse effectively and safely. A barn has to be large enough to provide shelter, access, and use, for the purposes at hand. So our minimum structure for a team of workhorses might well be more like sixteen by twenty-four feet in order to provide two stalls and a bit of room for a rack for equipment (bridles, harness, etc.) and a grain box.

The building block idea, deeply set in people's minds, is a tool of wonderful simplicity and flexibility. It is easily expandable. Once the single-crib barn or stable is built, wings and second stories can be added. Or it can take other forms that suggest different "types." The fact that the building block works so well is testimony to the ingenuity of the old carpenters and farmers.

Placing buildings into categories based on their structure pattern (form and floor plan) demonstrates their genealogies and helps us learn about transmission and evolution, sometimes through centuries. Form (floor plan, layout, height) is important because form is relatively stable through time and space. We can use form to devise categories that help us study patterns of diffusion, settlement, and other questions about local history. However, putting barns into a classification based on form is only a device of the researcher, because farmers and people who use barns tend to classify them by their purpose—horse barn, hay barn, granary, stable, hog barn, tobacco barn, and so forth.

(Above) Perhaps the most prevalent type of barn in Missouri is the transverse-crib type. This frame barn, seen with farmer DeLisa Lewis, is near Hatton. (Callaway County 2003)

(Left) This brick barn with trim and ornamental vent is on a successful farm near Stark. (Pike County 1974)

Most stores, roads, houses, mills, bridges, barns, warehouses, and so on take their form from the needs of everyday life, work, and commerce. A building type—floor plan, roof form, height—tends to be stable, and types can be traced across time and space. By charting the diffusion, or spread through time, of different types of barns, we can learn about the origins of barn forms. Some types of Missouri barns—the *English barn* being perhaps the clearest example—can be traced back to the Middle Ages in Britain and German-speaking Europe. So looking into the question of a barn type's diffusion is enlightening work, but in addition there are other forms that sprouted from the American landscape.

ORNAMENT

People choose building types and styles for many reasons. They may want a building to make an impression on the neighborhood, to express financial success, or participate in fashions of the day. Patterns in vernacular architecture may last for centuries, but they do change over time as social, economic, and technological conditions change.

Barns often display the style of the age, such as Georgian, Greek Revival, or Gothic Revival. These broad popular styles reflect national changes in taste. Stylistic ornament is applied as a suit of Sunday clothes, put on a building to dress it up. The style that "smarts up" a commonplace building is a vital element in the building's social and cultural context. And the application of fine details of style, which adds to the cost of the building, helps indicate the social status or relative prosperity of the owner.

(Right) The "old beef barn" at the University of Missouri-Columbia, the oldest public university west of the Mississippi (1839). (Boone County 2003)

(Below) Decoration may be part of construction, as in the handsome curve of a doorway and rendering of mortar joints in the sandstone mule barn at the Fulton State Hospital (formerly State Lunatic Asylum No. 1). (Callaway County 2003) Some barns suggesting new ideas—in function, design, or style—are built by institutions as experiments or as models pointing the way for others. Some are built with the latest style to reflect a company's success. Some are constructed with extra care and expense because the builders imagine the barns will be in use a long time; and perhaps to show the success and stability of an institution such as the State Hospital in Fulton.

(Far Right)In the late nineteenth and early twentieth centuries, several companies developed impressive manuals for barn builders. Many were able to offer detailed plans for a great variety of barns. Many of the barns, while based on very old floor plans and concepts, tried to speak to the well-off farmer who wanted to make a statement with an expensive "new" kind of barn. For example, the Radford Company, which produced a number of pattern books and manuals for barn building, advertised a "Pretentious Stock Barn" in their Radford's Practical Barn Plans in 1909.

(Below) A restaurant looks much like a high-end dairy barn (Eureka, Jefferson County 1992), perhaps with a hint of German-American half-timbering. Features of old barns can be employed in business and commerce in many ways. Companies use these elements to suggest "hominess" or "country" feelings. Restaurants may suggest comfortable stereotypes from former times, from not only the old-fashioned country store but from farm houses and barns as well.

Barns often reveal the process of how ornamental styles are used in commonplace architecture. Older barns were built and rebuilt by generations of pioneers. More modern barns are more influenced by trends in agricultural practices, pattern books, university experts, etc. Some of the new ideas cut the ties to honored local traditions in regions like the Boonslick, Little Dixie, the Rhineland, or the Boot Heel. Future generations will wonder what happened to the "old French colonial barns" or the "old tobacco barns" that were taken for granted way back in 2003.

Symbols are important. Symbolic features can become rooted and live on with new functions (perhaps simply of beauty) after their original purpose or belief disappears. Some families of German and Swiss ancestry appreciate a "hex sign" in the eaves of their barn, said to speak of ancient pre-Christian symbols and beliefs. Most farmers we know prefer to regard them as a fitting way to ornament a barn and give it character and added beauty.

Decoration on barns can serve practical as well as aesthetic purposes. Ornamental holes often called *owl holes* can be located in eaves of barns or over main doors. The holes allow owls, swallows, and other birds access to the barn, where they forage for mice and insects, helping keep the barn clear of the pests. Owl holes may be shaped many ways, and often are made by sawing adjacent parallel pieces of lumber so that they make a desired shape when nailed on the wall. Apart from practical functions of admitting light and ventilation to the barn, birds historically have been considered good luck in a barn. An additional function, the addition of a welcome decorative element, is also present in this simple detail of a barn's character.

Barns continue to appear in many media, of course. Images of an old barn and rural scenes have been used for magazine covers, calendars, television advertisements, and countless other uses for at least two centuries. The image sends messages

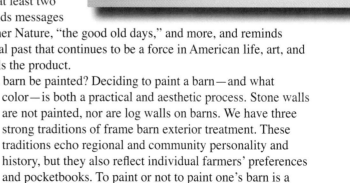

PRETENTIOUS STOCK BARN—A179
Cost of Blue Prints, $35.00

This pretentious stock barn is very complete and of an elastic pattern, so designed that its capacity can be increased by building on to the gable ends and extending them out any distance that may be required without affecting the general arrangement or exterior architectural proportions in the least. The two wings to

sort of court around the silo, admitting the sun, but obstructing the severe storms and giving shelter to the stock. The silo is well situated with reference to feeding, being in the middle of the cow barn. The cows stand back to back, which is of great advantage in cleaning out the gutters, as all the dirt can be handled from the center

SOUTH ELEVATION OF STOCK BARN

the right and left of the silo contain the young stock and horses respectively and face the south. These two wings form a

driveway and carried to the manure pits to the right. To the left hand or west end of the cow barn is a large room for imple-

of peace, harmony, Mother Nature, "the good old days," and more, and reminds people of the ancient rural past that continues to be a force in American life, art, and literature. The image sells the product.

What color should a barn be painted? Deciding to paint a barn—and what color—is both a practical and aesthetic process. Stone walls are not painted, nor are log walls on barns. We have three strong traditions of frame barn exterior treatment. These traditions echo regional and community personality and history, but they also reflect individual farmers' preferences and pocketbooks. To paint or not to paint one's barn is a choice that may be governed by individual ideas, adherence to family traditions and local habits, or simply by the availability and price of paint.

Barns may be left unpainted, allowing the fresh oak and pine boards to age naturally. Whether or not a barn is painted has nothing to do with the quality of construction. In early times, paint was very expensive and professional painters were few. Only after industrialization, availability of factory paints, and the growth of local painting firms in the later nineteenth century did barn painting become commonplace. Just as with the numerous guidebooks and manuals for carpenters and builders, books and magazines were published for the painters and stainers.

While many young men were recruited to help paint their family's barn, barn painting has long been a profession calling for specialized equipment and knowledge. Barn painting remains a profitable occupation today, with itinerant teams of barn painters using modern paints and paint sprayers traveling through the region offering their services to farmers.

Barns are usually painted red or white. The dark red "ox blood" color was called *sang de boeuf* (or *gros rouge*) and popular among French people and "barn red" has long been a favorite among upland Southern pioneers from Virginia, Kentucky, etc., as well.

Once the barn has received a coat of paint, which helps protect the wood and provides a degree of satisfaction and admiration, the barn will need to be repainted as time goes by, to preserve the wood and renew its appearance. Paint consists of the pigments or dyes (giving it color) and some kind of binder—the solid ingredients that hold the pigment particles in suspension. Problems with older kinds of paint arise from the toxicity of the pigment compounds (e.g., cadmium) as well as the lead, oil, alkyd, or latex resins making up the binding agent. There were paint factories in Colonial times, and by the 1860s, the first ready-mixed paints were becoming available with the growth of industrialization and mechanization.

"Barn red" paint was made from a mixture of red lead and linseed oil. The lead came as paste in a can, and one mixed it with linseed oil till it got to the desirable level of brightness and suspension. Though red paint was the cheapest, it lasted the longest.

White paint was more costly, involving more ingredients. White lead (lead carbonate) is mined from "tiff" ore (barite) in Missouri but is a more highly refined lead. Linseed oil, plus turpentine, was mixed in. White lead could be ordered from catalogs like Sears and Roebuck in one-hundred-pound kegs. Other natural pigments include colors made from ocher, chalk, and black graphite. Throughout the earlier years of the painting profession, the painter was in danger of becoming ill or even dying from lead poisoning—"painter's colic."

This transition suggests that the application of white paint to a similar barn could be an indication of several factors—the farmer having more money to spend on painting his barn, or perhaps as a kind of status symbol, or perhaps because his successful neighbors were painting their barns white. Or, painting a livestock barn white may speak to the later nineteenth century concerns for increased cleanliness in the milking process, because white symbolizes purity.

(Above) A familiar sign advertises Meramec Caverns on Interstate 70. (Callaway County 1998) Agreeing to let a company paint their slogan or ad on the barn may well give the farmer some extra income, in the same way farmers receive extra income from companies who convince them to erect billboards and cell phone towers on well-situated property.[3]

(Above) In the Loutre Valley of Montgomery County, this transverse-crib barn appears not to have been painted (note the gambrel roof, more expensive to build than a gable roof and more efficient). (2003)

(Far Right) Red transverse-crib barn on the prairie in Ralls County. (2003)

(Below) Well-maintained barns with white walls and green roofs add identity and distinction to a farm near Bay in Gasconade County. (2003)

(Right) The red paint has all but faded away on a barn in Montgomery County (note the mechanical loader to move small square hay bales to the loft). (2003)

Many people in the eighteenth and nineteenth centuries made whitewash (a mix of lime and water) for covering board fences (think of Tom Sawyer's legendary Hannibal fence) and walls of houses. Recipes for whitewash were handed down in families and available in books and magazines. Milk, rather than oil, was often a basis for paint. The least expensive method of making a structure white, whitewash nevertheless was not long lasting. The owner needed to reapply fresh coats on a regular basis to keep the fence or building looking good. Whitewash does not seem to have been common on barns in Missouri.

In these traditions of exterior barn color (white, red, or left plain), there is a lot of variation. Individuals with their own ideas may paint their barns differently, and so we find barns in light blue or gray or yellow. A well-known doctor in Foristell (Warren County) had his barn painted chocolate brown in the 1930s, and to achieve the color he wanted the painters mixed red lead and creosote. Barn colors help infuse rural Missouri with distinctive character and a palpable "sense of place."

Linseed oil–based paints replaced lead-based paint. Linseed oil is produced from flax seed and has many uses for the carpenter and craftsman. Now, water-based acrylic latex paint is rapidly replacing linseed oil– and soy oil–based paints, for several reasons; government regulations make oil-based paints more expensive and harder to manufacture under new ingredient controls, acrylic latex lasts longer, it resists mildew, emits less odor, and is easier to clean up.

CONSTRUCTION

Most barn builders learned their trade through apprenticeship and by imitating skilled artisans rather than through formal education. At the same time, barns exhibit changes in technology, and indeed the 150-year story of the Industrial Revolution is told in building a barn. New techniques and materials developed by engineers and architects found their ways to the barn builder's project—such as today's steel beams and panels and the much-appreciated air-powered nail gun.

Vernacular building often (but very rarely exclusively) employs local building materials. In early times, barn timber and lumber could be derived from the farmer's own woods. Many of the materials could be produced with axe, splitting wedge and maul, broadaxe, auger, mallet, and saw. Such tools, as well as a range of blacksmithing equipment, were part of the standard array in the farm shop. Other materials—nails, for instance, and door hinges and windows—could be acquired at the nearest country store, or, by the later 1800s, ordered from Montgomery Ward or Sears and Roebuck catalogs.

In most cases when we look at vernacular buildings, we do not know the specific builders and designers who contributed. Occasionally we learn about individual builders, and these occasions are always welcome and fascinating. Many elements in building a barn today are quite similar to old methods, and visiting with a crew putting up a modern pole building can give us a good deal of interesting information. However, the architectural record is incomplete. And while we are fortunate to have a wealth of houses built by French settlers along the Mississippi River south of St. Louis and in the range of hills as far west as Washington County, we have few farm structures clearly showing French architectural heritage.

By contrast, and logically perhaps, there remain on the landscape countless early buildings erected beginning in the later eighteenth century by pioneers from two distinctive groups. First there were the Virginians, Kentuckians, and Carolinians, etc., of British ancestry (*old stock Americans*). Many of these pioneers are identified as Scotch-Irish people and many of were Protestants in their religious orientations.

The second major group of farmstead and barn-building pioneers were families of German-speaking heritage, arriving a bit later. While many of these were from the *plattdeutch*-speaking areas of the northern German-speaking regions of Europe, many others were *Hochdeutsch* from southern regions along the Rhine and were as likely to be Roman Catholic as Protestant.

On some of our very old farms, barns remain that were erected by African-American builders who were part of the prevailing slave community in the century before the Civil War. Some antebellum farmhouses erected by slaves are now thought of as "old Southern mansions." Questions of design and construction are complicated in terms of African-American contributions, for we do not know the extent to which slave builders also did the design, site selection, and layout of buildings. In many cases there were highly skilled slaves with design roles as well as abilities to lay a stone foundation, hew logs, cut mortises, and piece the structures together in the best carpentry methods.

(Above) A neglected nineteenth-century barn that may well have been made of oak timber from the woods that was sawn into dimension lumber at a local mill, perhaps the farmer's own woods and mill. (Adair County 1989)

(Right) Contemporary pole barn of the same type (though it lacks a hayloft) assembled from prefabricated parts, 1989; walling and roof are prepainted steel sheets. (At the author's farm, Callaway County 2003)

FUNCTION

Nowhere is the old saying, "form follows function," more apparent than in patterns of the ancient barn. Barns take forms that reflect their uses and they are often given names that reflect these functions—hay barn, cattle barn, hog barn, tobacco barn, dairy barn, and sheep shed. Barns may have been built as strong boxes to hold and protect, but in almost every case the family or builder brought aesthetic traditions to the construction and decoration of this most practical of buildings.

A building's use can change comparatively easily. An abandoned farmhouse may be turned into a hay barn or grain bin. An old hay barn may be turned into a machine shed—or perhaps an antique shop, or perhaps rehabbed as a fine home in the country.

THE LITTLE RED BARN AND MODERN LIFE

The barn is a potent symbol in the cultural landscape of America. Today, few barns of the old make and mold are built. Barns may be subjects of admiration for their timeworn beauty as well as their often elegant modes of construction.

The building of traditional barns has declined, almost ending a two-thousand-year history from ancient Rome to Europe and Britain to America. The process of change began in earnest in the mid-nineteenth century with the spread of new inventions for mechanical harvest and storage of hay and grains, such as the McCormick reaper (1834). While sizes and arrangements of barn spaces provided space for the early machines, the huge diesel tractors, plows, planters, and self-propelled combines (with their various attachments) are too big for all but the biggest barns.

Barns have begun to move, at increasing pace, from the necessary shelter for livestock, crops, and machinery, to a status of curiosity and historic site. Compared with Missourians of a hundred or even fifty years ago, few people growing up today have a first-hand understanding of the insides of barns. One supposes this process is inevitable, given the drastic changes in rural living and the loss of the old farming community where families raised their own hogs, chickens, and cattle, with new agricultural practices and new methods by which we put meat and bread on our tables.

Farming on a massive corporate level means countless family farms and buildings are one by one being wiped out, along with the fence rows, patches of woods, and wildlife. People of long experience see these changes as inextricably tied to politics and the rapid growth of corporate business on local, state, national, and international levels. We must leave it to the reader to decide whether this kind of "progress" is, in the long run, a good thing for Missouri's future generations.

Once essential to everyday work on the American farm, the iconic nineteenth-century barn has become obsolete. Most old barns are neglected or altered if not indeed destroyed. The picture is not all bleak, of course. The concept of "barn" is deeply set in us, so when a person builds a garden shed or garage, the choice is often to put up something that looks very much like a real barn. We can buy the kit at the lumberyard.[4]

Barns of the future—will there be any? Certainly, but they might not look like the big frame barns and stables of our collective past. We will grow more and more reliant upon our community museums, historical agencies, preservationists, and a small number of very devoted farmers to hang onto our old barns for future generations. But there will always be a need for shelters to support and protect the hard work of the family farmers of Missouri.

Perry County barn in 2003. (Photo by Jim McCarty)

THE SINGLE-CRIB BARN

(Left) Ozark landscape with log single-crib barn, Texas County. (1991)

(Above) Terra Bella Farm single-crib barn serving as a garage and toolshed; the gable facing the west and the weather illustrates the American passion for symmetrical, balanced buildings. (2003)

(Right) The versatility of this building block is seen in another single-crib barn at this farm. This is a field barn, located well behind the other barns and dwelling, and it stands alone. It is situated with its doors facing south. In this instance, also from the nineteenth century, we see a log barn serving as a corncrib and a stable. The 6"–9" logs were left round and joined together at the four corners by the "saddle notching" method. As with many log corncribs, a frame shed addition was built at the time of construction. Here, the addition was put on the west side and made for feeding livestock. The log crib section is 10' x 12'6" and is set a foot off the ground on limestone pillars which support square hand-hewn sills. The square plates are also hand-hewn. Since the structure served as a corncrib, the logs are not chinked, thus allowing air to circulate inside the crib. With the addition, overall dimensions of this building are 24'6" wide by 12'6" deep. The crib and addition are sheathed in 10" sash-sawn yellow pine boards nailed flush.

I n deciding categories of barns, there are many options. Some name a building type by its exterior style or look. Here, though, we judge a building's type by examining its floor plan (or layout). The floor plan helps us suggest a barn's type, along with its height, opening locations, roof form. The floor plans of barns help us trace the heritage of individual barns, because the plan tends to stay the same over long periods of time and over great distances. Barns in Missouri are within inches the same plan as barns in England and Scotland.

In our typology we sort most of Missouri's historic barns into just three basic types: the *single-crib barn*, the *English barn* (with its several varieties), and the *transverse-crib barn*. There are countless permutations of these basic floor plans or types and it is interesting to see how builders work within traditions and still vary their own buildings to suit themselves or their bosses. A lot of different terms may be used for the same barn type, and some scholars develop specific types for practically any barn that looks different from the next one. The many varieties of Missouri barns are all shifts and extensions of the *single-crib barn* type, the basic building block—that square or rectangular one-unit structure we spoke of in the previous chapter. This is so for all American barns, and especially so in the southeastern United States, a significant source area for Missourians in the early times.

That single-unit stable or barn of one room (very often with an addition or two) is found across the state. The modest size of the structure may mean that some people just call the building a "crib," or a "shed." The fact that the single-crib barn form was the prevailing space for free-standing corncribs and granaries increases its interest, and also its complexity.

Let us visit a farmer in Callaway County, DeLisa Lewis. There is a typical nineteenth-century *single-crib barn* at Terra Bella Farm, where Lewis and Holly Roberson operate a farm that caters to specialized markets in Columbia and the St. Louis area. This single-crib barn was built on "the Red Dudley place," their 1880s farmstead on the rich prairie landscape on Auxvasse Creek of north Callaway County. The example here is built in frame and was laid out in a rectangle 34'2" across the front by 20'9" deep. The central crib, or rectangle of space, is 12' wide. The front of the building faces the east and the blacktop road, and the barn is part of an open courtyard arranged with other buildings and the white frame house typical of builders from Virginia, Kentucky, Tennessee, and North Carolina in this part of "Little Dixie."[1]

Its purposes for existence having faded with changes in the farm operation and other corn storage methods, the log barn at Terra Bella has seen better days. It appears now as a derelict in need of some tender loving care. Such corncribs in Missouri are virtually exactly like log corncribs throughout the upper South in Virginia, North Carolina, Tennessee, and Kentucky.

The rectangle is versatile. It most often had sheds or lean-tos built on one or both sides (sheds were added to all kinds of barns, of course). This is a small barn type, but the central space is easily enlarged.

The additive principle that infuses vernacular building and folk custom with

(Above) Log single-crib barn serving as a corncrib, V-notched hewn logs, Lincoln County, with an unsupported side shed roof seemingly typical in some German communities. (1988)

(Left) Log single-crib barn with additions, Cole County. (1974) Destroyed.

order and balance is seen in these farm buildings. Added onto sufficiently, the single-crib barn may become quite elaborate. It may have a log crib as its core, but be surrounded by frame additions as in this outstanding example in Cole County near Wardsville.

With construction of hewn horizontal logs so prominent in Missouri, we would expect to find a number of log single-crib barns. And indeed there are (well, were) many.

Log barns are founded on the essential *single-crib* plan and yet their additions give them more space. If two units were built end to end with a driveway between, the result would be a *double-crib barn*.

Endangered buildings are sometimes rescued to be reconstructed at outdoor museums. One place where good work is being done to study, conserve, and interpret historic buildings is Faust Park in west St. Louis County. A number of interesting

buildings have been sorted into a grouping that helps visitors understand pioneer life and architecture. At Faust Park, the William Schlueter barn, moved from its original site where it would have been destroyed, offers a lesson in what can be done to save and interpret buildings otherwise cast aside.

The Schlueter single-crib barn was used as a corncrib and equipment shelter. Logs are hewn flat on the inside and outside and joined at the

(Above) Added onto or piled up, as in this red frame granary in Warren County (2003).

(Left) The single-crib type can simply be a "slat crib" for ear corn (Boone County 1974).

(Above) This summer kitchen and two-level smokehouse/cellar in Audrain County (1974).

corners by the V-notching method. The central space—the log section—is sixteen feet wide by twenty feet deep. With the two side additions, in frame construction, the building measures thirty-six feet wide by twenty feet deep. Built in 1868, these logs measure from seven by fifteen inches to seven by eighteen inches in width. Like most

other single-crib barns, there is a gable roof, and like other corncribs, it is set off the ground on rock pillars to help protect the crop from critters. The sills are hewn square on all four sides, to provide perhaps a more stable base for the log floor joists supporting the building's floor.

(Left) William Schlueter barn, St. Louis County. One superb detail of this log barn, differing from most we have seen, but perhaps a theme representing this locality, is that the walls indicate the use of a foot adze for the hewing, rather than the more familiar broadaxe. (2003)

(Below and Right) similar log barns in their plan and functions, with the central core serving as a hay mow; hewn logs, Moniteau County; round logs unhewn, Callaway County (1974), while (Bottom) is a hewn log half-dovetailed single-crib barn of roughly similar size that has been covered with horizontal weatherboarding that suggests its purpose is something other than a corncrib or hay barn, Boone County. (1974)

WOOD, THE DEFINING MEDIUM

The majority of settlers who decided to cross the Mississippi River to stake out farms possessed basic skills in working timber and wood. Missouri was a frontier of timber. Apart from localized instances of stone and brick construction, which called for advanced knowledge and intensive labor, barns in timber frame or in horizontal or vertical hewn logs were prevailing forms of construction from earliest settlement.

The nineteenth-century barn required specific and demanding skills. Most pioneer-era people could help clear land, fell timber, mark off a square for a building. Many knew how to split shingles, slack their own lime for making mortar, even hew logs with a *broadaxe* or *foot adze*. Certainly countless cases exist where the pioneers built practically everything with their own hands, and with the help of a few willing neighbors. But more technical jobs like making mortise and tenon joints, crafting a mullioned window, laying up a stone or brick fireplace, or fitting roof trusses together were best left to experts.

After the early hunting and trapping days, there were carpenters and artisans who put their services up for hire. Specialists advertised barn-building expertise and made good livings by traveling through the community erecting barns for farmers on contract. Close examination of most old buildings offers excellent evidence of the difficulty and complexity of putting together a good quality "log cabin" or "barn."[2]

In the oldest surviving barns, two traditions of timber construction were used, both of them coming from the Old Country: the horizontal log wall (usually including log sills, joists, and plates), and timber framing (alternately called box frame, heavy timber, or post-and-beam construction). Both traditions were familiar on the European continent among French and German-speaking peoples who came to Missouri. In the British Isles, however, log construction was unknown.

In Colonial America, it is usually accepted that German-speaking immigrants, beginning in Pennsylvania and the valley of Virginia in the 1680s, taught the English and Scotch-Irish how to handle the broadaxe and hew log walls. British carpenters were familiar with the *adze*, but this tool differs significantly from the common broadaxe, the favorite log-hewing tool through much of pioneer Missouri. Germanic traditions of log building struck home with the Anglo-Americans. This form of horizontal construction, along with timber framing, became familiar in the early period.[3]

Included in timber framing were the two modes typical of England, called *half-timbering,* and its Germanic equivalent, called *fachwerk.* Timber framing employed the marvelous joinery of the mortise and tenon, called "peg construction" by many old-time farmers and builders. The French in early Missouri had their own version of log construction, in which hewn logs were placed vertically in the walls rather than horizontally. Taken with the mid-nineteenth-century evolution of *balloon framing*, which came with the spread of circular saws and cheap nails, those modes represent Missouri wooden barns.

It was not until German-speaking immigrants arrived in Pennsylvania in 1683 that broadaxe technology as we know it was introduced into the American colonies. German-speaking peoples adopted the common house types of the Anglo-Americans, however, and a beautiful product emerged that combined the old German woodworking technology with the Englishman's house: "the American log cabin." The American log cabin's shape and form derive from Britain and its log construction derives from Germanic Europe.

The key tool in building hewn-log buildings is the *broadaxe.* This is a woodworking tool sharp on only one edge. Like the chisel, the drawknife, foot adze, and froe (for making shingles, barrel staves, and splitting oak and hickory for baskets, chair seats, etc.), the broadaxe cleaves or splits wood away along the grain. In contrast, knife-edged tools—chopping or felling axes, saws—cut across the grain in any direction desired. The marks left on logs indicate telltale marks of the broadaxe (which leaves a scoring mark), and the carpenter's adze (which leaves a slight cupped depression in the wood).[4]

First, the carpenter uses a *chopping axe* (sharpened on both sides) to strike diagonally into the side of the log to the depth desired. Then, the hewer comes along after this *scoring* is done and uses the broadaxe to hew away the unwanted outside pieces to derive a rectangular-shaped log. The unwanted outside pieces or chips are the same parts of a log that are called *slabs* when a saw saws a log and leaves outer rounded pieces as waste. The top and bottom are usually left round, to make a closer fit and reduce the amount of chinking needed.

(Above) Mr. Wienhaus demonstrates hewing, first with felling axe to make his scorings, and then (Far Right) with the broadaxe he used to hew new oak sills to repair the barn.

(Upper Right) Weinhaus barn, Randolph County, a timber frame transverse-crib barn of the nineteenth century.

(Right) Oscar Keith, who remembered how to wield a broadaxe, painted a picture of the farm where he grew up, with log house and barn. (Audrain County 1974)

Near Mount Airy in 1974, farmer Louis Weinhaus described how, about fifteen years earlier, he replaced the hewn log sills in his transverse-crib barn by making new ones with his chopping axe and broadaxe after one of his mules had taken it upon itself to try to kick the barn to pieces.

The *adze* (foot adze, carpenter's adze, shipwright's adze) is another important tool in the old-time carpenter's chest. The foot adze was used for squaring timbers in timber-frame construction and in rough-planing planks and sawn boards for flooring. While the broadaxe seems to have been thoroughly accepted by log hewers across our state, there are instances where the log timbers show the distinctive "scooped out" marks left by the carpenter's adze.

Until quite recently, the broadaxe (and perhaps less frequently, the adze) were used on a daily basis for "hacking" railroad ties. Sometimes the tie hackers sharpened their broadaxes on both sides to make the work go faster. In certain parts of the state where there is good oak timber and a ready market, a person could convert an acre of logs into hundreds of railroad ties, offering an excellent source of income.

Corner-timbering methods in Missouri mainly fall into three styles, *V-notching*, the *half-dovetail*, and *saddle-notching*. Saddle notching ("saddling") is used when logs are left in the round, and often on less elaborate or meaningful structures. Other corner-timbering methods here include square-notching, and in rare cases, full dovetailing and forms of Scandinavian cornering.

Right along with the farmers' log barns and cabins, timber-frame construction was used by the first settlers as well. In timber framing, a bit more technical know-how was called for, because the mortise and tenon is the key to the construction, with squared pegs (*trunnels*) in drilled round holes locking the timbers and bracing together in a stout rigid box sheathed in protective siding.

Such barns are called pegged, due to the distinctive look of the whittled peg sticking out through the hole. No nails are needed in this ancient method of joinery. The pegs are carved squarish and tapered gently throughout their length. The holes are drilled with a twist auger, or later in the nineteenth century, with mechanical augers.[5]

Many of us are familiar with historic photographs of a barn raising, showing men and boys posing, tools in hand, at the rising skeleton of a hand-hewn pegged timber-frame barn from years past. By the late nineteenth century, the modern balloon frame system of lightweight framing based on sawn two-by-four lumber and making use of inexpensive wire nails, was replacing the older systems that relied on the use of the broadaxe, auger, and other tools of the ancient carpenter.

In Warren County, a nineteenth century *single-crib barn* formerly used as a granary, now being dismantled, offers a look at this framing technology. In this instance, the building includes both hand-hewn timbers and timbers sawn out at a mill. Like the majority of historic farm buildings, we see a transition in these buildings. During the nineteenth century, farmers witnessed the change from heavy post and beam construction to building with light sawn members (often called balloon frame) held together with nails. By the time most of the barns were built, sawmills were able to supply dimension lumber. (See photos at right)

(Right) A gallery of hand tools pulled from a carpenter's chest would include: Left to right: One-inch forming chisel (which could cut mortises), hand auger for boring holes, gimlet (to make small holes for starting nails and screws in difficult wood), a variety of chisels, try square, boxwood caliper rule, double marking and mortise gauge, different kinds of saws and screw drivers, bevel (this one home made), set of wing dividers, and folding pocket knife (that belonged to the author's great-grandfather Robeson). For many a child in days gone by, the old carpenter's chest was a treasure trove. Tools included items like measuring devices and ladders, but on the conservative side we may say it would take something like twelve tools to build a frame corncrib, including floor, roof, and hinged door. If the sills and plates are hewn from trees instead of being sawn, add a broadaxe or adze to the list. If the framework is to be joined by the mortise and tenon method, add augurs, chisels, and mallet. (2003)

(Far Right) One of the hallmarks of the old-time carpenter was "tricks of the trade"—traditional methods of building found in no book. Billy Lee of Wright City, master builder, violinmaker, and woodcarver, demonstrates the technique used by an old German-American barn builder he recalls in Warren County. The old gentleman held up his watch and chain to get his vertical lines plumb. Lee uses his father's South Bend railroad watch to show how the old-time carpenter derived a vertical line. The watch becomes the plumb bob. (2003)

(Below) In the hills of Cole County, an impressive bank barn reflects the quality of the land for row crops as well as fine cattle. (2003)

ARRANGING THE FARMSTEAD

Another way to look at the design and uses of barns is to consider how farms were laid out. Farmstead organization is worthy of its own full study.[6] The land is shaped and cultivated, with graded agricultural spaces, orderly margins of protective and symbolic fences, ponds, roads, trees.

The problem of making the best use of one's property has different solutions. With today's diesel-powered machinery, it is hard to appreciate the enormity of gritty labor it took 150 years ago to clear stumps with an axe, grubbing hoe, shovel, and team of oxen. In some places, the job never ends; every year it seems like the same rocks have to be pulled out of a field and thrown to the fence row.

Sometimes the land clearing and shaping was radical, as in the clearing of the Ozark forests for timber and the deep plowing of bottom lands and native prairies for crops. Sometimes land on its way into production was less obvious, as traditions of grazing livestock on prairies, savannahs, and "cedar glades."

In Missouri, we inherit three basic farmstead layouts: the *linear plan*, the *L-shaped plan*, and the *U-shaped* or *courtyard plan*. So to some degree agricultural landscapes continue to show the conditions of settlement generations ago. In many cases, terrain and individual needs meant some farms lacked careful organization, but most farmers put their buildings together in a logical pattern that made for an orderly, predictable daily routine. While we like to try to categorize farm plans, in reality there is immense variety and blendings of patterns.

In the *linear plan,* house and barn are aligned with the front of the house and the barn or stable doors facing south or southeast. The *linear plan* goes back to European farms where domestic space is adjacent to and often attached to spaces for a dairy, a cattle shed, horse stable, and crop barn. Farmstead organization responds to topography. The linear plan often places the lane and the buildings along the base of a hill, to make the fullest use of the more level fields, prairie, or bottom lands.

(Above) Cedar glade and "blackjack flats" landscape near Yukon, Texas County. (2003) In parts of the southern Ozarks, a cedar glade (as my guides Ed McKinney and Cliff Bryan showed me) is where there is an outcropping of limestone and lots of moisture, with red cedars growing in clusters on poor farmland. The sandy loam soil is thin there and farmers hit bedrock less than a foot down. Fence posts could hardly be driven into the earth. The land in creek bottoms is the best cropland, and some of the open uplands have been made productive. One area is known as "the blackjack flats" because of the frequency of tough blackjack oak. Cliff Bryan of Pomona (now living in West Plains) grew up in this difficult landscape and recalls, "You couldn't raise hell on it with a gallon of moonshine and a red-headed woman." (March 2003)

(Left) Linear farm plan in an Anglo-American area, Callaway County. (1992) One stereotype we encounter, in terms of different communities, is that Anglo-Americans and Scotch-Irish from Kentucky, Tennessee, and Virginia tended to prefer the linear farm plan. In fact, all three principal Missouri farmstead plans (linear, L-shape, open courtyard) are common in the British Isles.

(Below) L-plan farm, Audrain County. (1974) The L-shaped plan, perhaps the most common farm layout in Missouri, puts the farmhouse facing the road and the assemblage of other buildings and barns in a ninety-degree angle going back from the house.

The U-shape is convenient in utilizing space and making easy access to different buildings, and it was favored by many farmers with sizeable and successful operations. The open courtyard plan, found in many parts of the world, represents the ultimate in farmstead organization of the Age of Improvement in the eighteenth and nineteenth centuries. The open courtyard or U-shape plan offers balance, order, and symmetry. The central courtyard, usually positioned facing south or southeast and surrounded by the house, barn, and structures such as chicken house, woodshed, machine shop, smokehouse, garden shed, etc., has ancient antecedents and parallels in farmstead layout going back to Roman times.

(Right) Near Edinburg, Grundy County; citizens renamed the town from Buck Snort in hopes of attracting the railroad, but to no avail. (1990) In other instances, also to some extent the "luck of the draw," farmers in northern Missouri on the prairies—distant from major cities and commercial centers—might find themselves in a handsome, rich agricultural landscape, as in parts of Grundy County.

U-shaped or courtyard layouts: (Below) in Howard County's hemp and tobacco country that drove Missouri's economy in early times (1974), and (Right) in the extraordinary Femme Osage valley, where Daniel Boone had the good sense to settle (2003). The U-shape or courtyard plan is the third familiar plan used by pioneers in Missouri. This pattern has a long history in Europe and Great Britain and indeed other parts of the world. It groups main buildings around a central space, typically behind or next to the dwelling. But in Missouri, the courtyard may be thought of as an open courtyard, for it is not entirely enclosed. There are distinctions between the typical large farmstead of the old British pioneers in Missouri and their German-speaking neighbors. One interesting feature is that on the British farmsteads the house tends to be the most prominent feature and usually at the front and facing the road. In contrast, on many of the early German farmsteads, the house is less obvious and often located further within the group of buildings; often it is the large hay barn that is the most prominent and visible feature from the road.

One important factor in settlement history was simply who arrived first and who had the knowledge to make the land work. Those who had first crack took the best land, and later pioneers tended to move into areas with lesser reputations for land, such as the inner Ozarks.

For the barn builder and user, working within the flexible framework of inherited traditions that do allow new ideas and technologies, the land defines the puzzle of what to build. Climate, landforms, nearby construction materials—such as quality hardwoods like our pines, oaks, black walnut, and hickories—and many other ingredients in the process of building depend upon the land.

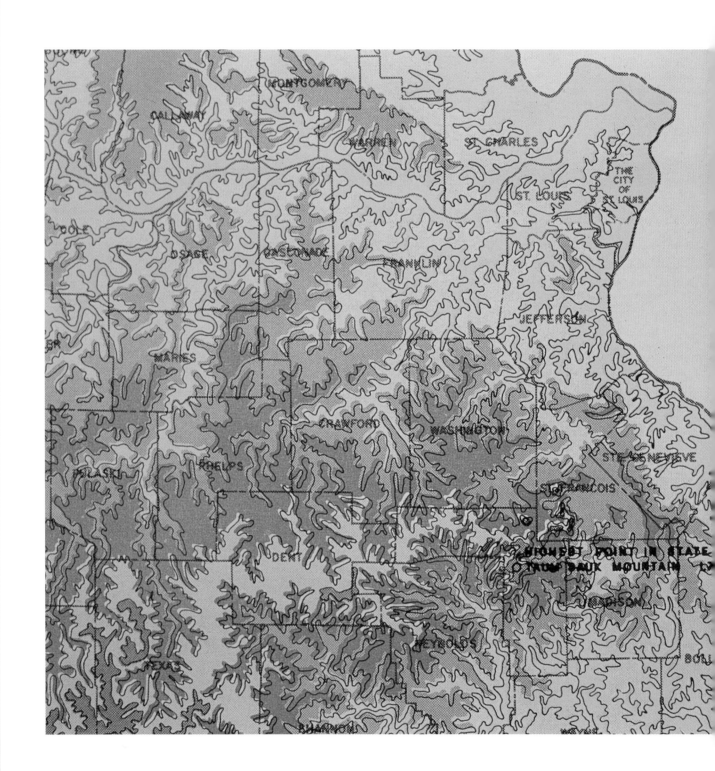

BARNS OF THE FIRST EUROPEAN FARMERS: THE FRENCH

4

The French were the first European settlers in what would become the state of Missouri. They brought buildings and culture to the Ste. Genevieve district of colonial mining and farming settlements in the eighteenth and early nineteenth centuries, before the waves of Anglo-Americans and then German-speaking peoples. While dating buildings is technically demanding and often impossible, many agree that buildings remain from the eighteenth century, but the old barns, if any, have been lost.

The old French settlements were for the most part confined to the banks of the Mississippi and Missouri Rivers and their tributaries from above Cape Girardeau to St. Louis. Among the early settlements were New Madrid, Cape Girardeau, Perry, Ste. Genevieve, New Bourbon (a Royalist French settlement), Mine La Motte, Old Mines, Racola, Carondelet, St. Louis, Florissant, St. Charles, La Charette, Labadie, and Cote Sans Dessein. Most began as fur trading posts and shipping points along the rivers. After 1760, the French gave the lands east of the Mississippi River to England and the west side to Spain. Soon after the Louisiana Purchase (1804), Anglo-Americans began to acquire property and land; speculation in mining, forests, and agriculture changed the economy and way of life.

This area experienced many problems with land ownership, boundaries, etc., especially after American ownership and surveys using the American township and range survey system. People tended to stay in clusters of older houses and gardens despite the American surveys which tried to change the shape of properties. Village life continued here, with numerous small settlements in the woods and along creeks, connected by trails and small roads that can quickly get the outsider lost.

The French village pattern, inherited from Normandy via Canada, features long lots running back from the long central street, the street parallel to the river or creek. Thus, Old Mines evolved organically, tuned to the topography, roads, mines, and cattle-droving roads through the forest. In Ste. Genevieve, farms were separate from the town and its dwellings; farm workers walked to and from "the big field" (*le grand champ*) each day, and kept their horses in stables in town. In the Old Mines area, people lived on small farms and only did part-time farming and mining.

The pattern is still visible in Missouri towns and countryside. Its unit of measure was the *arpent* ("acre," equivalent to about one English acre). The official system of French "long lot" land division came to North America with the first Acadian settlers. There is some confusion about its precise dimensions.

(Left) "Land Relief Map of Missouri," 1980, indicating Mississippi River from Cape Girardeau to above St. Louis, and Missouri River from St. Louis to Jefferson City area. (Courtesy Missouri Department of Natural Resources)

(Upper Right) French long-lot land division is clear in maps such as the 1848 Hutawa Atlas showing both sides of the Mississippi just south of St. Louis.

(Lower Right) Map of St. Louis town lots in 1804 by H. E. Rice Jr. for a diorama in the Jefferson National Expansion Memorial, 1958; we get an impression of farm layout and hints of barns. (Peterson 1993)

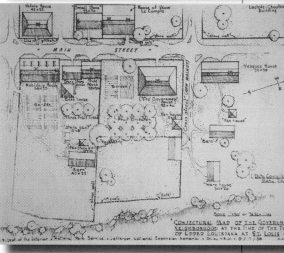

In the Old Mines and Racola community, only a few places have open and relatively level areas where the habitants could develop corn and wheat fields. The rolling and steep eastern Ozark hills are difficult terrain, where large deep outcroppings of flints, sponge rocks, and sandstones prevent their removal. Most of these farming areas were in the bottom lands along the more gentle slopes beside streams. And each of these fields, where we now see abundant if small pastures and crops of hay, were made fertile only by first removing by hand the millions of rocks covering them.

So in the "mineral area" of the Ozarks, farming tended to be small-scale and subsistent. More than farms, people here had large gardens that supported their needs. While they developed few substantial farms, the French were famous for the excellence of their gardens. Every *cabane* had a large garden, the small outbuildings to support it, and typically a small barn with enough space to feed horses and mules and store small quantities of hay and livestock feed. The French kept horses and mules for the seasonal agriculture necessary to keep a small farm going. They had a milk cow, some hogs, and various guinea fowl and chickens.

It may be that no huge barns were built in the earliest period, since there was little need for them. The French customarily let their livestock roam the woods until needed at the farmstead. By doing that, the animals foraged on their own, making large fields and hay crops unnecessary.

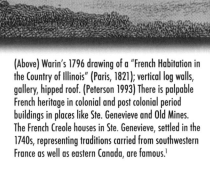

(Above) Warin's 1796 drawing of a "French Habitation in the Country of Illinois" (Paris, 1821); vertical log walls, gallery, hipped roof. (Peterson 1993) There is palpable French heritage in colonial and post colonial period buildings in places like Ste. Genevieve and Old Mines. The French Creole houses in Ste. Genevieve, settled in the 1740s, representing traditions carried from southwestern France as well as eastern Canada, are famous.[1]

Contracts for house and barn construction appear in the old French archives. For example, a "barn of white oak posts 40 feet long and 22 feet wide, roofed with shingles or with bark and with a threshing floor" was built in Ste. Genevieve in 1792, and these specifications indicate a three-bay "English" threshing barn virtually the same as the medieval French *grange* or barn.[2]

(Left) Louis Bolduc House, circa 1793, open for tours and reconstructed to suggest its character, furnishings, and garden in the colonial period. (1979)

One clue that the saga of French barns is complicated is seen in the Victor Javaux barn south of Perryville in Perry County. Today this area is known more for its 1830s and 1840s German-speaking immigrant farmers, but in the early 1800s French families lived here, including French who came to establish farms. The Javaux barn was photographed in 1937 as part of the Piaget-van Ravenswaay Survey of the Historic American Buildings Survey, one of President Franklin D. Roosevelt's Works Progress Administration programs. WPA photographers, artists, architects, and writers

(Two Photos Below) The immensely important J. B. Valle barn stood at the corner of Main and Market Streets in Ste. Genevieve. (HABS photograph circa 1940) This barn was owned by Jean Baptiste Valle, a leader in the French community. It suggests European (but also British) multipurpose barns and stables of 250 years ago. The French who farmed the "big field" and the common fields in the bottom lands and Mississippi River flood plain around Ste. Genevieve had barns, but none seem to have survived the devastating floods and toils of time.

(Upper Right) Victor Javaux barn, circa 1830, Perry County, photographed 1937. (Courtesy Historic American Buildings Survey) We are tantalized by the view of the outside, which suggests that a stone two- or three-bay threshing barn may lurk just out of view. The form is right for such a barn, and this is the sort of barn that we believe would have been familiar in early French times.

(Below Right) Ten-dollar bank note issued by the Bank of St. Louis, 1817, when St. Louis still had French vernacular buildings; this is the oldest known illustration of St. Louis buildings. (Courtesy Joe Lindell, St. Louis) The structures which may be barns give little indication of anything distinctly French. In the foreground, the walled garden does seem French, and the small buildings may be barns.

worked in Missouri during the Great Depression, and a number of important buildings they saw exist for us now only in their records.

At the Javaux site, there is a shrine erected by French Catholics in 1851. Victor Javaux was a Christian Brother, and two of his brethren had apparently come from France to Ste. Genevieve in the 1820s to establish a school, but without success. The group decided to disband, finding themselves on the American frontier. Victor Javaux moved south to Perry County, married, and developed a farm on the "king's highway" (*el camino real* to the Spanish) running from New Madrid to Ste. Genevieve.[3] Today the king's highway is U.S. 61. Javaux built a fine stone house with a brick addition, in the tradition of prevailing American house types of this period across Missouri.

French barns may have looked much like the "English" barns common at the time among most groups of European-American farmers. The French barn was essentially the same plan—three bays, with large opposed doors in the middle, where the threshing and winnowing floor (*batterie*) was located. The big doors on the front were aligned with the ridge of the roof.

Details that would suggest French carpentry and custom may not be visible from outside. Several surviving French Creole houses exhibit the roof framing system brought by carpenters carrying forward methods from southwest France (if perhaps by way of Canada). Among the more familiar architectural features that might help identify French *granges* are a four-sided hipped roof and vertical log bearing walls in the French traditions of *poteaux sur sole* (post on sill) and *poteaux en terre* (post in ground). Many of the earliest buildings had thatched roofs, and the steeper pitch helped repel snow and water from the perishable roofing material.[4] In addition, the French also built log buildings with horizontal logs (*piece-sur-piece*), which may appear to be like other American buildings unless small details are studied.

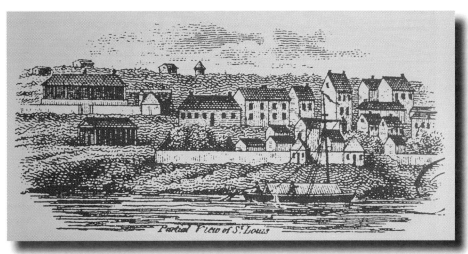

OLD MINES

For the place where Missouri French traditions still flourish, and where the old language may occasionally yet be heard, we visit Washington County. For the French in villages like Old Mines and Racola in the interior hills west of Ste. Genevieve, mining was the principal way of life in the early era. The Old Mines area of Washington County displays more French traditions than any other Missouri community.

Most of the first farmers only became full-time farmers later when conditions allowed. If fact, there were few full-time farmers, because the land was just too difficult, flinty, and poor to support the kinds of farms we see in other regions of Missouri.

Three hundred years later, the descendants of those old French families—sometimes referring to themselves by the somewhat clouded term, Creole—remain in the villages and on the land their forebears settled. Adding complexity to this group of people is the intermarriage of Native American with the French, resulting in what many call Metis cultural identity. And because many of the early French came from provinces in Canada, they may call their heritage French Canadian, to make things even more confusing. In early times the ability to hold a conversation in the French language distinguished the Missouri French, or Creole, population, but as time passed the language began to erode and fade.

(Above) Chapman Coleman house, (HABS 1937), typical *cabane* of the late eighteenth and early nineteenth centuries, with large stone central chimney for the cooking hearth.

(Left) Behind the Chapman Coleman house is a 10' x 12' round log saddle-notched *granary* (corn crib). The two kinds of notching dominant here are saddle notching and V-notching. (2003)

(Below) Ray Thebeau's grandmother and grandfather, Achan and Bridget Thebeau with some of their children and grandchildren on the porch (gallery) at their log house circa 1930 in Old Mines: row 1, Nora, Tom, Joe, and behind are Mrs. Bridget Boyer Thebeau and Achan Thebeau, Rosie, Toby, Mary Jane, and baby Noah Jake Boyer. (Courtesy Ray Thebeau)

Mining began around Racola and Old Mines in the 1720s as French entrepreneurs were given vast land grants in Upper Louisiana by the Spanish. One of the principal areas was called "La Vielle Mine," the term for the Old Mines and Racola area of present-day Washington County.[5] The French hoped to find silver but instead found lead. Even today, heavy nuggets of raw lead ore can be found in the creeks. The ore was shipped to smelters and river ports such as Ste. Genevieve.

Among the early settlements in the eastern Ozarks lead mining territory were Mine a Breton, Racola, and Old Mines. Racola was the earliest village of the Old Mines Creoles. Old Mines became more prominent when St. Joachim Catholic Church and village of Old Mines were established a few miles south in 1820.

The main crop on the better bottom land here was wheat, and much of it was shipped to Ste. Genevieve and from there to New Orleans. While Ste. Genevieve, the political and economic pivot for the French communities, had relatively large cattle farms and dairies (*vacheries*) and saltworks, this was not the case in La Vielle Mine.

Ray Thebeau, from one of the earliest Old Mines families, says, "We spoke what they call the brogue French," (March 2003) unlike French taught in schools. Ray's wife, Mary Theresa Merseau Thebeau, stopped speaking French when they were sent to school at age nine in 1941. A few terms, such as *grange* for barn, *poulailler* for the henhouse, *cabane a mahis* or *appentis a mais* for corncrib, *four* for oven, *cabane* for a horizontal log cabin or house, may be recalled by some members of the older generation such as Mr. and Mrs. Theabeau upon reflection. But such terms, including the term *Creole* (preferred by scholars for the early generations of American-born French people), are mainly familiar to people active in studying and preserving local history, as well as those participating in the Rendevous and re-enactments.[6] Among other important survivals of early French culture among the Missouri French-Americans is the annual New Year's mumming ritual called "the *Guignolee*," in which celebrants go from house to house singing and playing music in expectation of receiving treats from the residents.

There seem to have been two main kinds of barns here. First, there was the *granary*, a single-crib log barn with shed additions on both sides. In French, the added lean-tos or sheds seem to have been called *appentis*.[7]

Most of the Old Mines log barns still standing and in use date from the early twentieth century. If a barn is relatively large and primarily for loose hay floor to ceiling, as in the Charlie Pashia barn, it is called a *pole barn*—or sometimes a *log barn*. But if a barn is in the form of a small single-crib barn with its central space for feeding horses and mules and its flanking rooms for grain and shelter, it is called a *granary*.

Typical measurements for the single-crib *granaries* are fourteen by fourteen feet for the central crib (usually of log), with ten to twelve-foot shed additions on the sides. Almost invariably the roof type here is the gable roof. In Old Mines, there seem to be none of the massive hewn timber roof systems in the ancient Norman truss system familiar from colonial and early buildings in Ste. Genevieve. In fact, none of the Old Mines barns inspected in our research seem to date before about 1850.

The central crib of the *granary* is where horses and mules were fed, with a small hayloft above. A shed addition on one side, usually left of the stalls, shelters a wagon, equipment, and gear. The shed addition on the right side is floored and walled inside with vertical sawn boards and here is the actual "granary" where corn is stored. These wings or shed additions are for storing ear corn, which is shelled off the cob for livestock feed as needed.

In some cases, as in the old log *granary* of

small round oak "poles" at the Ed Pratt place on Arnault Branch, the shed addition has been recently chinked in the old French manner, called *bousillage*. The chinking, which consists of grass with the damp sod attached and straw, gives weather protection to the horses. In this important structure, the livestock-feeding wing was added on the north side of the log pen by the most recent occupant, a 1950s German immigrant named Graves.

The second type of common barn was the *pole barn* (*grange de boulin*), which in form is a single- or double-crib barn but with frame additions around the central crib/bay built with "poles" (small cedar or white oak trees, hewn or left round). There were, of course, other kinds of barns, but these two kinds seem to best represent the community in this part of Missouri.

Here, the central section of the *granary* and the *pole barn* typically is made of unchinked round white oak logs ("poles") six to eight inches in diameter and "saddled" (saddle-notched) at the corners. The old French term for logs left round was *en boulin*, and this method of building in horizontal log became common after the influx of Anglo-Americans in early nineteenth century.

(Above) Charlie Pashia farm. Early French maps say, "this is where the best farm land is." This is among the original Spanish land grants. Located in the Rabbitville community on the Salt Pine branch of Old Mines Creek, various members of the Duclos and Pashia families have lived here for many generations. Farmers along the creek bottoms had the best soil, though every field had to be cleaned of rocks, a process that has never ended. While the farm appears isolated after construction of modern highways, in early times it was connected by trails and small roads to other settlements, farms, and the mines.

(Upper Right) "Spesh" Coleman's single-crib *granary* near Charlie Pashia's farm, with horizontal log walls, no chinking, and gable roof, circa eighteen feet square, with framed additions for livestock feeding and grain storage. Leaving spaces between the logs allows the ears of corn to dry and receive ventilation. (2003)

(Two Photos Right) Bill Pashia barn, a *granary* type expanded in size. This is a large rendition of the single-crib barn (granary) type and has an interesting story to tell. An interesting detail is the unusual pattern, for this area, of the forged-iron door hinges. Were these on the lumber and older doors from a barn in Maine, or built from scratch by Pashia? If the lumber was already made into a barn, taken apart and shipped to Missouri, the hinges could have been made and installed in Maine. Pashia may have liked the pattern and started making hinges for new barns around Old Mines in that pattern. It was made from 2.5-inch fir lumber apparently shipped from Maine via the upper Mississippi River and St. Louis, and either reassembled here or built new here in the 1920s. It is said that the lumber and timbers are decking and framing taken from a salvaged naval vessel. The construction is like nothing else in the area—old mortise and tenon joints in heavy, hewn fir beams. The form of the barn is typical of the older *granaries* with large loose hay storage in the middle, and flanking additions for grain storage and livestock feeding. The barn has a 1920s roof in the then-popular gambrel shape, and lean-to additions for horse stalls, and was specially built by Mr. Pashia to add volume to the central core where loose hay was stored. The owner, Bernadette Bequette, appreciates this barn's importance in the history of the community.

The *pole barn* is a logical extension of the same single-crib granary concept. Sometimes, in more substantial instances, the pole barn may be made of two large log cribs. Returning to Charlie Pashia's farm, there is the single-crib *pole barn* with a horizontal round log central crib circa eighteen feet square. This large single crib, where loose hay was stored, is surrounded on three sides by frame additions with vertical poles for uprights and rafter pairs (with half lapped joints). A "pole" in the Old Mines region is a skinned white oak or cedar tree (left round or hewn square with a broadaxe) approximately four to six feet in diameter. The white oak logs are *saddled*, the term in this region for "saddle-notching."

This is an area where the broadaxe is still known, and log buildings continued to be built by conservative farmers and perhaps economically challenged farmers well into the twentieth century, and perhaps even into the twenty-first. None of the log barns (granaries or pole barns) we visited were painted originally. A few log barns have received coats of red paint on their frame walls in recent times, and one or two 1950s-era large hay barns are painted white.

Building in log or frame was a decision based as much on economics as tradition. In this part of Missouri, the raw materials for a round log structure could be obtained and the basic structure erected at modest cost, if the builder could handle an axe and a dozen or so tools. And log houses, barns, and corncribs were built to last. While many scholars insist on describing such buildings as "impermanent" and "temporary," we beg to disagree. The majority of log barns and many corncribs were covered with protective siding at or near the time of construction, just as were log houses.

(Two Photos Above) Charlie Pashia log single-crib barn. Two mechanical hayforks for loading loose hay hang from the steel track in the gable, one over the original crib and one over the adjoining framed-in open bay that appears to have been a later addition. (2003) The actual granary and livestock feeding mangers are in the surrounding frame additions. There is a gable roof, as on most of the earlier barns across Missouri.

(Left) Selby Warden farm: hay barn. (2003) In the Cruise (Bliss) community overlooking Old Mines Creek, the large hay barn was built with vertical cedar posts in a single-crib plan. The central open space was entirely for storing hay, floor to ceiling. Walls and additions for grain storage and feeding livestock were made of horizontal split-cedar palings as siding material, and these palings may be a reflection, albeit faint, of ancient French methods.

(Three Photos Below) Charlie Ross log double-crib barn and farmhouse, Cruise community. (2003) This area was blessed with superior cropland. The older term for this kind of pole barn, still used by some residents, was grange de boulin ("barn of poles").[8] Walls are horizontal laid, saddle-notched, white oak logs four to six inches in diameter left in the round. The roof system is simplified sawn bracing with two- by four-inch rafters. The barn is what researchers usually call a log double-crib barn. The size of the house (built in an Anglo-American plan and design) reflects substantial farming operations.

(Photo Right and Photo Center) Roy Essmeyer barn, and framing system of sawn timbers. (2003) In the Aptus community, a large red frame hay barn focuses on a central bay entirely used for loose hay. Grain was stored and livestock fed in the side areas, so its form is essentially what many French-Americans would call a granary. For the researcher, however, the barn is in a category called transverse-crib barns.

The gambrel roof represents a late nineteenth century turning point in barn construction as the standard gable roof became old-fashioned. Though the gambrel roof type occurred earlier, its widespread use was only possible after the introduction and acceptance of balloon-frame construction, inexpensive manufactured nails, and innovative uses of truss construction. The gambrel roof helps date barns to the early twentieth century (assuming the barn has its original roof), when this practical roof shape became popular across Missouri.

The gambrel form allows better protection from the weather with its steeper roof lines that shed water better, and provides substantially more space under the roof for loose hay. Furthermore, the use of the large trusses meant that there were no crossbeams above floor level in the hayloft, which meant that the new-fangled mechanical hayforks and hay harpoons attached to steel tracks in the peak of the roof could be used to rapidly and efficiently load great amounts of loose hay in the loft.

(Right) One of the major mid-twentieth-century barns is on the Branham Bequette farm in Racola; its gambrel roof and size make it commodious by comparison with other barns here. (2003)

Ms. Lucy Alma DeClue's 1940 frame *granary* in Racola, a small single-crib barn, sports a gambrel roof. Ms. DeClue's father, Wilfred Pashia, built the barn and blacksmith Bill Pashia forged the distinctive D-shaped iron hinges. (2003)

In a small and physically secluded community in southern Madison County lies a group of farms established beginning in 1799 by French farmers in the fertile bottom lands along Twelve Mile Creek. This area, south of the Zion community, has a number of substantial general-purpose barns, typically in the transverse-crib plan. The dwellings here are much like standard Anglo-American types and only slightly suggest Creole houses of the early period. In our brief survey of these barns, thanks to the advice of Bill and Patricia Holmes, we observed features which may (or may not) mark them as French.

One element potentially French is the use of horizontal weatherboarding to sheath exterior walls of these barns, an unusual feature in Missouri often marking very early construction. But horizontal weatherboarding was commonplace in early Virginia. Another feature, noted by Van Ravenswaay many years ago, is the large "bonnets" ("hoods") covering haymows on some of these barns.[9]

Hay bonnet enclosing the haymow door and hay-loading track in transervse-crib barn near Brewer in Perry County. (2003)

Barn on Twelve Mile Creek, Madison County: Double-crib. (2003)

The large bonnet over the haymow is common in this area and south and east into counties such as Wayne, Perry, and Cape Girardeau, but rare in other parts of Missouri. Some of these barns have an attached corncrib or granary on the other side of a cross passage. Thus, we have a set of barns that may or may not represent French influences in an agricultural community, and these barns deserve future study. Until future study, it is too early to define the large hay bonnet as French.[10]

Costner barn with projecting gable supported by vertical posts, south of Twelve Mile Creek, near Lodi in northern Wayne County, 1920s. (Courtesy Missouri State Archives)

THE THREE-BAY BARN: THEME AND VARIATIONS

Three types of barns were dominant in Missouri from early settlement across the nineteenth century and much of the twentieth. To some extent, these barn forms symbolize their early connections with peoples essentially of English, Scotch-Irish, and German-speaking origins across the Atlantic as well as "Back East" in pioneer source states of the U.S.A.

One of these types, as we have seen, and especially in the French-American settlements of the eastern Ozarks, is the *single-crib barn*. The second of our three basic types comes from the Old World and is familiar in the Upland South as well as Pennsylvania and other places of German emigration—the *three-bay threshing barn*, with its principal varieties called *English barn*, *log double-crib barn*, and *bank barn*.

The *three-bay threshing barn* or as many call it, the *English barn*, is the continuation of barns of antiquity. The form is defined as a barn with its main entrance along the side and aligned with the roof, and with two cribs separated by a threshing floor (or hallway/driveway) running between them. This barn is typically built on level ground. Between two cribs (bays) for hay or stabling, the central bay was often provided with a floor. Usually there is a hayloft above the main floor.[1]

American colonists built three-bay threshing barns in New England and down the

(Left) "Barnyard scene," 1910, Kimmswick (St. Louis County). (Courtesy Missouri State Archives)

(Right) Textbook example of the three-bay threshing barn, or English barn, DeKalb County. (2003)

East Coast. In earlier barns, the central bay was for threshing grain, and later for the convenience of loading hay from wagons and storing equipment between two working bays. Numerous examples throughout the British Isles are precisely the same in form and use, except that, over there, the construction material is more likely to be stone or brick.

THE ENGLISH BARN

As a term, *English barn* reflects its type (form), but not its real history, because the *English barn* type is predominant in many Scottish, Scotch-Irish, Irish, and German-speaking communities in Missouri that scarcely have English heritage. In German regions, particularly if built on a slope with a stone basement for livestock, we are accustomed to calling it a *bank barn*. This discussion reminds us of how complex is history. Barns cannot be easily pigeonholed. Like the people of our state, cultural versatility and complexity are the hallmarks. There is, as always in folk tradition, variety within the type. The *English barn* type (sometimes called *double-crib barns* in the literature) takes many variations and nuances.

The English barn type has its limitations. Primarily a barn for threshing grain and storing hay because it is on one level it has limited areas for stabling and feeding animals. Its cousin, the *bank barn,* solves the livestock problem by instituting a basement area for the animals. The English barn reflects its use in places where livestock were few and generally housed in a separate building (called a *byre* for cattle and *stable* for horses), and where the storage for wheat or hay was more modest.

(Above) English barn type? (Cole County 2003). The photograph from the road may fool us; the hint of a sloping site suggests that if we got inside the barn it may need to be classified as a bank barn. The small, unsupported roof (pent roof) on the north (left) side, shelters livestock and appears often in German-speaking communities.

(Right) Barn on the Governor Frederick Bates farm in a modified English barn plan. (Lower Far Right) Its interior partition is beautifully made of 21" to 22" vertical cottonwood boards and the tell-tale parallel marks of the sash saw (up-and-down saw) are visible.
(St. Louis County 2003)

(Above) The typical older English barn proved unsuitable for large dairy operations in the Midwest. But the type could be modified. An example along old U.S. 40 in west St. Louis County, threatened by encroaching development that now surrounds it, was built not of frame or log but of ceramic tile block. (2003)

(Right and Bottom) Three-bay English barns were often called "Yankee" barns in heavily Southern Little Dixie, but the distinction seems to have applied mostly to examples in frame construction. Yankee barn is probably a later nineteenth-century usage. (Right) In northeastern Macon County, on the northern edge of Little Dixie, Ben Cook called his barn a "Yankee barn" in 1974. It measures 37'6" across by 30'6" deep, and the center driveway is 12' feet wide. (1974) (Bottom) The layout of this barn gives us a sense of typical English barn floor plans. (Marshall, *Folk Architecture in Little Dixie*)

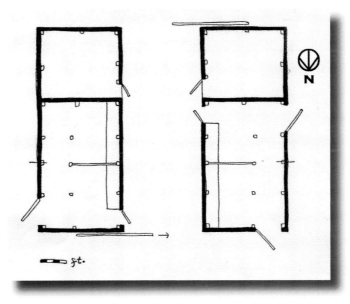

By the time Missouri was settled, *Anglo-American* substantially meant British Isles–based people from the South, with many families containing small but distinct veins of German-speaking heritage. Among these groups, it is perhaps the Scotch-Irish whose vernacular building heritage made the greatest impression in terms of farm buildings. These were the people of the Colonial Tidewater and Piedmont Upper South, and then of the Tennessee Valley and the Kentucky Bluegrass. Of Anglo-Saxon and Celtic backgrounds and coming from sharply different parts of the British Isles, they were often to become thought of as English or Irish on the frontier. Catholic Irish as well as Anglicized Scots, Welsh, and Cornishmen were lumped together with the English, while the Protestant Ulster Scots were lumped together with the Catholic Irish. Eventually these communities became linked into the French-speaking people who were here before them, and the many German-speaking immigrants who generally came after. It was the predominantly Protestant British-style people who came to be thought of as "Southerners."[3]

Missouri offered much to the British, Europeans, and old-stock American settlers. It was microcosm of the frontier and exemplified American ideas—not least of which is opportunity for penniless or landless fellows to claim a piece of land, no matter how small. Although this is extremely simplified, let us look at a region generally considered to be decidedly British in its imprint—Little Dixie (and its subregion, the Boonslick). It is perhaps in the Boonslick and Little Dixie where early Anglo-Southern traditions are most apparent and long-lasting.

Little Dixie is a classic community of Anglo-Americans.[4] This large region in central and northeast Missouri saw the development of economic and political influence in the decades after statehood and before the Civil War. The region features soils suitable for the two main crops before the Civil War, hemp and tobacco. Little Dixie's actual confines in terms of counties has always been somewhat foggy. Many disagree as to which counties it contains; it is a "folk" region that lives in people's memories and traditions as much as in more tangible elements. For this writer, the counties in Little Dixie include Pike, Ralls, Marion, Monroe, Shelby, Audrain,

(Photos Above) The design of the W. L. Cornett barn, 1884, Linn County is considered inefficient for 2003 purposes, so it is under review for demolition. The timber framing and mortise and tenon construction are of the highest caliber. (1986) The barn was built in Linn County by a family whose people had come to Missouri from Virginia, Kentucky, and Tennessee in the 1830s and 1840s. The framing includes modern nails; this combination is a transition from older technology to emerging technology of nails and lighter lumber. The Cornett farm was given with a vast collection of furniture, personal documents, textiles, and more, to the University of Missouri–Columbia's College of Agriculture by sisters Winnie and Bracy Cornett.[2]

(Right) Near California, Moniteau County. (2003)

Callaway, Boone, Randolph, Howard, and substantial parts of surrounding counties such as Lewis, Lincoln, Chariton, Carroll, Linn, Cooper, Saline, and Lafayette. We would also add bits of Montgomery, Macon, Cole, Osage, and Moniteau. The clearest border is to the east and south, where the Missouri River and the German-speaking settlements strongly mark different areas of history. Like all true folk regions, the borders are hazy and identity of the region depends on local traditions and interpretations.

(Below) Bright red English barn in Crawford County with gable additions. (2003)

The region is located in the north central and northeastern section of Missouri, bounded by our two great rivers—the Mississippi on the east and the Missouri on the south. Like other cultural regions, Little Dixie simultaneously displays elements of its heritage and elements of continuing cultural changes in its range of vernacular buildings. It is surprising to see a region of strong Southern architectural and Democratic political identity in northern Missouri, but such is indeed the case. This is the area of heaviest settlement by upland Southerners, especially slaveholding farmers, in the twenty to forty years before the Civil War.

Even larger in terms of acreage is the Ozark region, an exceedingly complex place where the old British Isles cultural heritage, and most especially Scotch-Irish traditions, remains distinctive, with strong German settlement along the northern and eastern Ozark borders. Few regions are more misunderstood, or more complicated culturally, than the Ozarks. This vast region appears to take up most of the state from its eastern hills along the Mississippi River across the southern edge of the Missouri River and south to the Arkansas line, not including the Boot Heel and the prairies along the Kansas line north of Joplin and Carthage.

One of the ways the Ozarks seem to differ is in politics and the exact source areas for the Upland Southern emigrants. Most of the Little Dixie and Boonslick settlers came out of the Tidewater and Piedmont areas of Virginia, Kentucky, the Carolinas and Tennessee, while most of the Ozark settlers came from the mountainous areas (the Blue Ridge, the Appalachians).[5]

There are pitfalls in branding elements of American culture to specific ethnic groups. Even for the early nineteenth century and even for groups coming straight from the Old Country, the process of blending, cross-fertilization, and assimilation were pervasive in Missouri farming communities no matter how seemingly insular or isolated.

Along with the *single-crib barn* and the *transverse-crib barn*, the *English barn* type, ubiquitous in the Old Country and in many settlement areas in America, is one type in our attempt to categorize Missouri barns. Discussing this barn type brings us to the bog of complexity and lets us look at some extraordinary examples of the barn builder's craft. Numerous German examples exist in Missouri that remind us of two facts: the *English barn* form is versatile, flexible, and open to different kinds

(Above) An English barn is prominent in a cluster of buildings on a farm in the eastern Ozarks as the hills approach the Mississippi River in Cape Girardeau County (2003).

(Left and Lower Photos) In the upper Ozarks of Gasconade County we find an excellent example of the English barn of heavy timber frame construction. On the same farm is another early three-bay threshing barn with mortise and tenon construction, with a similar large square-hewn oak summer beam as other barns in the area. Hand-wrought square nails, wide vertical board siding (either sash sawn or riven), and stone foundation are often found in early examples of this kind of barn. This is one of those fascinating parts of Missouri where Anglo-Americans (and a few French) settled in the earliest phases, but where a great influx of German-speaking immigrants in the 1830s and 1840s very broadly became the dominant community. On the same farm, is this timber-frame English barn exhibiting the finest building skills. The granary next to the barn has had concrete poured between the vertical studs for insulation and protection, and the original lapped horizontal weatherboarding indicates its age. (2003)

(Right) Quite unusual in Missouri are painted symbols on barns. This red barn is embellished with a white star. (St. Charles County 2003)

(Photos Below) The Kotthoff barn in Gasconade County, in van Ravenswaay's 1977 documentation of German buildings and material culture in Missouri; he characterizes it as an "Upper Bavarian" barn,[6] a tradition that has the first floor made of stone and the second level wood. Built in 1868, the 90' x 30' barn has added interest due to its heavy timber frame construction with stone nogging (infill), called Fachwerk. This ancient carpentry tradition, employing mortise and tenon construction and massive hewn beams and braces with the spaces filled with insulating material, is a vital element in some of Missouri's German-speaking communities but rare among Anglo-Americans (though commonplace in England, where it is called half-timbering). Everything about the Kotthoff barn pronounces quality. In 2003, the barn's framework looks overbuilt, but the Germans built with an eye toward permanence. The barn faces south and house in this open courtyard plan. Fachwerk construction with stone nogging is visible under the front porch of the house. Hewn timbers and stone nogging inside and in the hayloft. (Photos courtesy Osmund Overby 1972) The barn was set upon a relatively level spot and no "bank" was needed. But if the slope were greater, it would be called a bank barn—reinforcing the difficulty of trying to classify vernacular buildings.

of construction techniques and variations. And secondly, some German-built examples in Missouri exemplify the legendary extra work and attention some German-speaking immigrants gave to their barns.

Historic photographs and archives give us enticing glimpses of important buildings lost to the ravages of time. Among these are two splendid German-built English barns in eastern St. Charles County. This bountiful farming area is among the fastest growing places in Missouri, with very rapid development and urbanization—so much so that eastern St. Charles County has become a simple suburb between greater St. Louis and Wentzville, where an automobile plant has drawn numerous new residents. Each day,

new highways, housing developments, and commercial businesses are laid down over one of Missouri's most interesting historic landscapes. Old buildings are rubbed out in growth areas like this all across the state. Losses of early barns such as these two examples, drawn from many destroyed barns recorded in archival records and memories, should sadden every citizen.

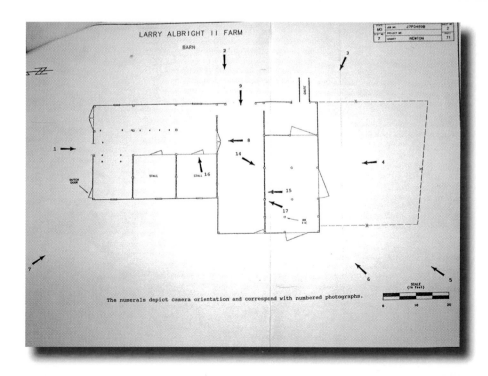

LARRY ALBRIGHT II FARM

BARN

The numerals depict camera orientation and correspond with numbered photographs.

A similar picture emerges in Newton County at the Bushner barn, recorded as part of a Missouri Department of Transportation (MoDOT) corridor study. Built in the early twentieth century, the barn generally has the plan of an English barn type but it crosses over different types. An outstanding sample of the old art of timber framing, it has added interest of horizontal siding. Its hayloft indicates the anticipation of installation of a modern mechanical hay fork that slides along a steel track in the peak of the roof, so a clear path through the roof beams is necessary. (Bottom Left) Plan. MoDOT conducts corridor studies or environmental studies to consider alternate routes for potential highway improvements, so staff document numerous structures and sites not impacted or altered. (Courtesy Cultural Resources, Missouri Department of Transportation, Jefferson City)

(Photos Above) What type is it? (Left) Near Farrar, east Perry County. (Right) Dudley "Model A garage" near Hatton, Callaway County. (2003)

(Left) Lost Missouri. Duebbert barn, eastern St. Charles County; if we could see it now, we might find much of importance inside.

(Lower Left and Below) Even more painful was searching in vain for the Freese barn in eastern St. Charles County, destroyed by highway construction. This early nineteenth-century barn contained splendid timber framing, sections of *Fachwerk,* and a carved lintel with memorial words in the German language. Both of these barns were photographed by the Piaget-van Ravenswaay survey in the late 1930s and photos are available in the Library of Congress.

THE AMERICAN LOG DOUBLE-CRIB BARN

One of the once-commonplace variations of the English barn is the *log double-crib barn*. To the visitor, these archaic structures, usually in a sad state of repair, seem like ghosts from deep time.

A permutation of the three-bay threshing barn, long the staple of European and British people in America, the floor plan of the *log double-crib barn* is virtually identical to the *English barn*, but built of horizontal logs. This log barn is merely two *single-crib barns* built side by side with a drive between them. Log double-crib barns also seem to have been called *English barns* or *Yankee barns*.

The "old Ed Sapp barn" is located in Boone County in the old Kentucky and Virginia cultural hearth of Little Dixie, north of the Missouri River. The log double-crib barn is emblematic of this cultural region. The Sapp barn's log walls are joined by the omnipresent V-notching method. Its standard cribs, based on the ancient European sixteen-foot bay, have the driveway through the center, and the log sections are encompassed by frame additions. Since the log cribs have their own doors facing the hallway, unlike the English barn, there is no need for doors on the front of the barn. (Top Right) Front; one of the additions is almost gone, with only a bit of framing intact. (Bottom Right) Driveway for unloading wagons. (Top Left) V-notch cornering, with wide gaps between the logs to enhance ventilation for the crop of loose hay in the sixteen- by sixteen-foot crib. (Above) While hinges and nails were bought, the rest of the log crib and door was made on site with traditional tools; methods people have to build door latches are ingenious. (1974)

(Photos on This Page) Another example of a keenly functional log double-crib barn emerged from the overgrown wayside during a MoDOT field study in Benton County. In the Drennon barn we can see half-dovetailed hewn log cribs across the driveway. In this case, the doors to the cribs both face the front, rather than facing inward on the central driveway. The haymow function of the larger west crib is apparent from the gaps between the logs, and the granary function of the smaller east crib is apparent from its inside board sheathing. (Left) Haymow. (Below) Granary, (Below Left) Plan. (Courtesy Cultural Resources, Missouri Department of Transportation, Jefferson City)

The Christian Bergt barn in the Frohna area is located in a region settled by Saxon Lutheran immigrants in east Perry County. Led by Pastor Martin Stephan, some seven hundred Lutherans left Saxony seeking religious freedom and arrived in St. Louis in 1839. The group bought some forty-five hundred acres in east Perry County in and around the villages of Wittenburg, Altenburg, and Frohna. Among their first buildings was a log cabin for their college in the village of Dresden, and the college later became Concordia Seminary in St. Louis. The Bergt log barn, log house, and other buildings have been developed as a memorial to

the Saxon Lutheran pioneers at the urging of Charles van Ravenswaay and under direction of preservation consultant Gerhardt Kramer. It cannot yet be concluded that the barn was built by the Bergt family because the area first was settled by Anglo-American farmers from Kentucky and Tennessee. Before Christian Bergt acquired the farm, it was owned by Anglo-American pioneers named Twyman.

LOG BARN FLOOR PLAN

EAST CRIB

WORK BENCH (3'-10" x 7'-6")

WEST CRIB

FEED TROUGH

CRIB DOOR

2'-11" DOOR

STALL DIVIDER

6'-8" DOOR

TIN ROOF

TIN SIDE PANEL

Notes:
1. Logs in walls of cribs are 5" in width (across) and 6" to 7" in depth.
2. Building rests on stone blocks (8" above ground level).
3. Second door in west crib is 6' above floor (not shown in floor plan).

LEGEND
= Wood Siding
= Log Walls

Floor Plan for Log Barn.

(Photos on This Page) The half-dovetailed hewn log barn on the Twyman/Bergt farm is some 40' by 48'. Bergt built a frame structure around the original log barn circa 1900. (Right) Hay loft. (Photos circa 1978, courtesy Missouri Preservation Program, MDNR, Jefferson City) The Bergt barn is typical both of Anglo-American and German-American log double-crib barns in the early pioneer period, and perhaps future research will establish more details of its biography. One element here that does appear to be typically German-American is the tendency to retain older structures on family farms, and for this trait we are thankful.[7]

The log double-crib barn epitomizes the early settlement period in Missouri, yet it was so logical and deeply traditional that the form continued to be built well into the twentieth century.

The roof systems on these early log barns are made from lighter hewn timbers, or sawn lumber. Rafters are set in couples and almost always made of small skinned poles (usually with the top side hewn flat to receive the nailed roof decking), or of sawn lumber. Most rafter systems in Missouri feature half-lapped joints at the peak (mortise and tenon construction or nailed). In some cases there is a ridgepole to which the rafter couples are nailed.

One of the oldest places settled by Anglo-Americans from Kentucky is the Jim and Karen Marschel "Pumpkins and Pines" farm on Dry Fork in southern Warren

County. This farm's story suggests the succession of settlement (and types of barns) in nineteenth-century Missouri. The farm is situated in the old French territory where French villages were fleeting. This beautiful valley on the Missouri River tributary Charette Creek was a few miles from the French village by the same name established circa 1763.

The village has disappeared and the Anglo-American (or "English" as many German-Americans say) town of Marthasville, the oldest town in Warren County, was built near its location.[8]

The farm was part of one of the legendary Spanish land grants. In this case, the land was given to David Kincaid, "the pioneer Spaniard." Kincaid apparently did no building or farming here, and in 1803 he sold the property to John Wyatt, a Kentucky veteran of the Revolutionary War. Wyatt seems to have been the first permanent settler

(Above) An example in Callaway County suggests how complicated such a simple building can become. The old Binckley barn in the Missouri River bluffs is built of oak and walnut logs, round and V-notched. Later, a small crib was added across from the south gable, and a new roof extended to butt against the gable of the larger V-notched structure. A V-notched corncrib was finally included across a passage made next to the larger structure. Essentially, this barn is made up of several individual log barns organized together to make a larger and more versatile barn. This offers an excellent glimpse of the additive principle at work, where traditional spaces are added in a familiar, logical pattern that solves the farmer's needs. Again we are reminded of the wonderful versatility of the old-time carpenter who knew how to handle timber and tools. (1974)

(Center) Half-dovetailed 12' x 18' corncrib with shed additions on three sides. The crib is set on mortared stones high enough off the ground so that hogs can get under the structure from the south side for protection from the weather, especially in winter.
(Osage County 1974)

(Left) In Osage County, the Boekmann barn suggests variations on the log double-crib barn theme. The farm is in a community in the "Rhineland" region known for its German-speaking heritage, south of the Missouri River. But this barn is much like the Little Dixie Britisher's log barn, only larger. The logs are left round and V-notched at the corners. One of the cribs is the usual 16' square, but the other is some 16' x 20' and the central driveway is 22' wide. Also like Little Dixie versions, the log cribs are positioned on stone piers at the corners and stress points under the floor system. The German Catholic builders, organizing this farm around 1840, included other log buildings in their assemblage of structures to support life and work—including a half-dovetailed hewn log corncrib, a V-notched hewn log summer kitchen, smokehouse, and the main dwelling itself, which is square-notched. Such farms appear similar to each other in central Missouri, whether built by Scotch-Irish or English or Germans. Often the differences between log barns, for example, are subtle and may only be detected under close examination. (Osage County 1974)

in this part of the Dry Fork Valley. Wyatt "proved up" the land during the Andrew Jackson administration in 1835.

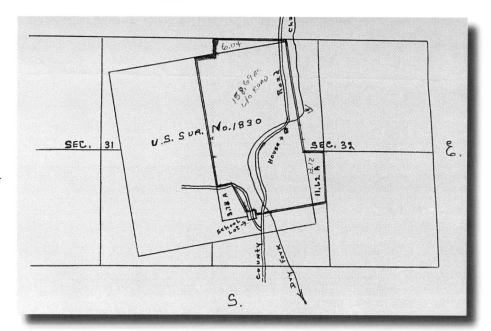

The Kincaid Spanish land grant is indicated on a plat book, notable by lack of orientation by the American survey system. The number "1830" refers to the number of the survey, not the year.

Wyatt's brother Anthony had come to buy the land in 1803, finally moving his family to the property in 1880. Apparently the brothers owned the property together at first, but John eventually became sole owner. John Wyatt moved from Kentucky in 1817, and began building the farm and clearing the land. John Wyatt became prominent in the region and held the first county court at his farm. Wyatt died in 1855 and was buried under an apple tree that grew from rootstock he carried in his saddlebags from Kentucky in 1817.

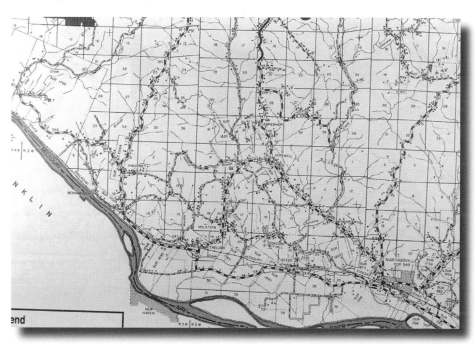

The farm is seen in a slightly off north-south rectangle with "SUR 1830." The county road map shows the rigorous checkerboard "township and range" land division dating from early United States possession of the region. Older French and Spanish land grants still appear on modern maps and can be detected in most cases by odd shapes and boundaries that do not coincide with "true north" surveying of the U.S. system.

An aerial photograph shows the farmstead's organization and lay of the land. The Wyatt-Marschel farm occupies the center and edges of the long narrow Dry Fork Creek Valley. In these valleys there is limited tillable acreage, so farmers have to find ways to survive economically. In 1989 the Marschel family developed "Pumpkins and Pines," a tourism destination for seasonal events. In the autumn, they sell pumpkins for Halloween, their corn maze is ready to be explored, and on toward Christmas, they sell Christmas trees the family has planted and tended. In the spring, they host Easter season weekend getaways to give children a taste of country life. This appropriate shift from farming to embrace "agritourism" helps families find ways to stay on the farm during changing economic times.

Among the numerous improvements they made to accommodate visitors was refurbishing the original *log double-crib barn* that dates to the John Wyatt era. Examples like this one deserve our notice and conservation efforts.

Aerial photo, circa 2000. (Courtesy Jim and Karen Marschel)

Looking at John Wyatt's story, we may propose its construction to have been around 1835. The barn's details reflect barns like this built from the eighteenth century into the twentieth century in regions of Missouri with plentiful hardwood timber. While it is commonplace to say that a particular person built a barn, we rarely know for certain whether or not a specific owner was the builder, or took part in the labor, or hired the work to be accomplished. In the age when barns like this were erected, most owners, if living on site, took an active role in design, layout, and often construction. The hardwood timbers came from the property or a nearby woods. Certainly someone on the construction crew (perhaps the owner) was skilled with the broadaxe.

The logs were joined at the corners by the traditional V-notching method. The walnut and oak logs, hewn on the inside and out, measure from six to seven inches wide by eight to twelve inches in height. The sills were hewn eight inches square and positioned on stone piers to provide a stable base. The passageway is twelve feet wide.

In these double-crib barns, there was a hayloft above. Also typical of early barns (and houses as well), the roof system features pairs of small logs (poles) hewn flat on the top to receive decking and shingles. Rafters are joined in the half-lap joint.

Originally unpainted, the Wyatt log barn, measuring some 41' x 40', was painted red by Jim Marschel when the change was made to "Pumpkins and Pines". Marschel added the porch and enclosed the open rear shed in 1988 to accommodate visitors' comfort.

(Right) Log double-crib barn and home built by Kentucky emigrant John Wyatt, circa 1835. Plan shown below photo. (2003)

Detail (above) shows V-notching corner method. (2003)

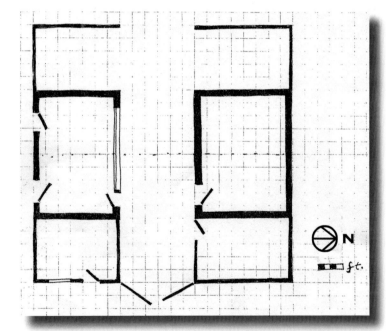

N

ft.

The old southern type house in 2003 retains much of its original 1878 character. (2003)

In addition to the historic log barn, here is an outstanding example of a more modern kind of barn. This is a 1911 transverse-crib barn, typical of later phases and introduced by Anglo-American farmers from Kentucky, Virginia, the Carolinas, and Tennessee. (Left) A lapped splice joint unites sections of the summer beam supporting the hayloft floor system. (2003)

Across the creek is another barn on the Marschel farm. This is a somewhat unusual barn because it lacks a passageway between the livestock spaces. Here, apparently for a dairy, there are two bays for cows, with milking stanchions. Above is a vast hayloft. Covered with corrugated metal siding, this frame barn from the early twentieth century features an impressive central vertical post supporting a beam, which in turn supports joists for the floor of the hayloft. Most details of its construction, with the exception of the central post and summer beam, are the same as those in the 1911 barn. In this barn, the timbers are black walnut, hewn square with a broadaxe, but the rest of the timbers and lumber are sawn at a mill, and the barn offers a look at the combination of older timber frame technology with emerging sawn lumber technology. A lapped splice secures the beams to complete the horizontal timber supporting the loft. (2003)

In Missouri, there was a shift from reliance upon log construction to a preference for frame construction in the middle of the nineteenth century. Early log barns, built as a convenient choice from nearby timber, tended to be replaced with frame or stone barns in the second or third generation. As more and more sawmills were built in towns and on larger farms and as milled dimension lumber was becoming available at lumberyards in railroad towns, frame construction became the method of choice in most Missouri communities.

Log double-crib barns are often not detectable from the road. Those with logs visible may be of recent vintage (lacking refinements present in early barns) or barns reassembled at history museums. Some history museums seem to prefer leaving the logs uncovered, probably so the logs are easier to see, but without weatherboarding or protective roofs the logs deteriorate.

(Below) The farm also has a log *single-crib barn*, built here as a corncrib. This 8' x 16' corncrib is made of 5" to 7" hewn oak logs. It becomes "Santa's Cabin" and other uses during seasonal tourist event weekends.

First-generation double-crib barns. (Top) Cape Girardeau County (2003). (Middle) Phelps County twentieth-century log barn. (2003) (Bottom) Fourt barn, Texas County. In a book called *This Old Barn*, Mildred Melton wrote, "Our log barn was built by my grandfather, Lewis Fourt, around 1880 on land my great-grandfather homesteaded about 1830 . . . this land has never been owned by anyone other than Fourts." (Photo by Ed McKinney 2003)

THE THREE-BAY BARN,
CONTINUED

THE BANK BARN

Another barn type that migrated across the Atlantic is the two-level *bank barn*. The plan of the main floor is that of the three-bay threshing barn, *English barn*, and *log double-crib barn*. What gives the *bank barn* its identity is location on sloping ground.

Following European tradition in northwest England, many parts of German-speaking Europe, and in Switzerland, *bank barns* work beautifully where the farmer's landscape necessitates accommodation to the undulations of hill and valley. A *bank barn* glories in the hillside. As two-level barns, the down-slope side of the structure works perfectly for a stone or brick foundation for the lower level. Common in Maryland, Pennsylvania, Delaware, New Jersey, and Virginia, *bank barns* became one the most frequently built barn forms here.[1]

The lower level, often carved into the side of the hill, is where milk cows, horses, oxen, and mules are handled and fed in the winter. Facing south or southeast whenever possible, the "basement" provides excellent shelter. The upper or main floor serves much as it serves in other three-bay threshing barns—threshing floor with grain and hay storage spaces on each side and above. The threshing floor, in examples well placed on the side of a hill, is reached quite easily from the uphill side. Grain and hay can be pushed down to feed the livestock below, enlisting gravity as a fellow worker.

In the many cases where farmers found themselves on flat prairie or creek bottom ground, as in much of northern and northwestern Missouri, builders provided a ramp up to the main floor (threshing floor). Sometimes the ramp is a mound of earth, sometimes a wooden bridge.

In Missouri's many-layered saga of settlement and agriculture, we have an impression that the English and Scotch-Irish tended to move quickly to adopt another type—the *transverse-crib barn*, that came from lowland Tennessee and Kentucky. (We look at this barn type in the next chapter.) We also have an impression that the *bank barn* retained its dominance, at least through the nineteenth century and half of the twentieth century, among early German-speaking immigrants and Missouri Germans.

That is a whopping generalization. We offer it based on several decades of observing barn types in different Missouri communities. In parts of Missouri where the frame *English barn*, the *log double-crib barn*, and *transverse-crib barn* are most prevalent—for example, Little Dixie, north Missouri, and the upper and upper eastern Ozarks, many people just call *bank barns* "German barns." But the *bank barn* is not typical in the bulk of the Ozarks hinterland of south Missouri and Arkansas. There, the transverse-crib form is dominant.

Some German-speaking immigrants came in family groups going back to 1700 after having been in Pennsylvania or Illinois for generations. Some groups came in what historians call "waves of immigration" during moments of tremendous political and religious stress on the Continent—the 1830s and 1840s—when carefully organized immigration was planned and carried out, as with the Saxon Lutherans in Perry County and the Philadelphia Settlement Society that founded Hermann in 1836 and 1837. Some groups had strong leaders, common goals, and financial resources, and set about forging a "new Germania" on the frontier.

The immigration societies were able to purchase large tracts of land from Anglo-Americans in what would come to be called the "Missouri Rhineland," generally south of the Missouri River east of Boonville and along the Mississippi River from St. Louis south to Cape Girardeau. The success of some of these German communities would eventually cause friction when some of the older populations were displaced. By the Civil War, many Anglo-Americans and French had lost their land through shifts in

(Top Left) Near Jefferson City, Cole County. (2003)
(Middle Left) Near Calumet, Pike County. (1974)
(Bottom Left) Near New Melle, St. Charles County. (2003)
A cluster of fine stone barns in this important region deserves extensive study.

(Above) The basic bank barn can become elaborate and large, many spaces added to the essential block (including adding a silo in the structure). Such ample, multipurpose barns serve more purposes than the kinds of individual buildings more familiar back in Europe. Gasconade County, in a heavily German-speaking community. (Photo by Jim McCarty 2002)

(Left) An example in *Fachwerk* (half-timbering) barn with mortise and tenon construction, at the restored 1839 Pommer-Gentner House in Hermann, part of Deutschheim State Historic Site. (2003, with site administrator Bruce Ketchum)

economy and politics and the impact of German settlement in their old villages like Ste. Genevieve and St. Louis.

Arriving in numbers in the 1830s, many German-speaking people found the land to be a blessing and a challenge. The land that seemed best for row crops was, for the most part, on the north side of the Missouri River and was taken up by the earlier Anglo-Americans, for tobacco and hemp crops. Some Germans found good land in the smaller prairies and bottom lands. For those from the lower Rhine Valley and upland regions of Europe, the hill country of the northern and northeastern Ozarks borders proved to be familiar and suitable. For those fortunate enough to understand the potential markets for winemaking, in Hermann, for example, those steep northern Ozark border hills were excellent.

(Photos Above and Left) Bank barns in Westphalia and in Freeburg (Osage County). (2003)

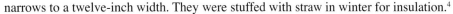

Sutterer, a German Catholic farmer, had the luxury of good nearby limestone. The barn measures 44' x 32'6" and has a central door and threshing floor, with livestock stable area in the basement. The wooden framing structure is of high quality, with heavy square-hewn timbers (9" x 9" posts, 9" x 12" plates and tie beams). No wooden pegs are visible, and the huge timbers are fitted together so that no nails or pins are necessary.

(Above) Joseph Sutterer bank barn and plan, Perry County, circa 1840, a fine example, yet with its own character.[2] (2003)

(Far Right) Bay Mercantile stables; Bay is a Germanic cultural landscape with interesting buildings, including houses of Anglo-American types. (Gasconade County 2003)

Rare in Missouri are ventilation slits or air vents. Such openings as holes or tall narrow openings like these provide illumination and air circulation to help cure the hay or fodder inside. Slit vents are common across the British Isles and Europe, where they have been used for several hundred years. Vents are more important on stone buildings, where ventilation was more difficult to achieve because of the density of the stone walls. These slit vents measure four by thirty-seven inches outside and the inside narrows to a twelve-inch width. They were stuffed with straw in winter for insulation.[4]

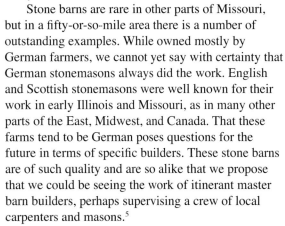

Stone barns are rare in other parts of Missouri, but in a fifty-or-so-mile area there is a number of outstanding examples. While owned mostly by German farmers, we cannot yet say with certainty that German stonemasons always did the work. English and Scottish stonemasons were well known for their work in early Illinois and Missouri, as in many other parts of the East, Midwest, and Canada. That these farms tend to be German poses questions for the future in terms of specific builders. These stone barns are of such quality and are so alike that we propose that we could be seeing the work of itinerant master barn builders, perhaps supervising a crew of local carpenters and masons.[5]

(Photos Above, Right and Far Right) The Linneman barn, circa 1845 on Puncheon Creek, built by Jurgen Linneman and sons Henry and Fritz, remains part of a working family farm. The original stone house was destroyed, but the barn was saved.[3] This three-bay, three-level bank barn is arranged on the side of the hill so the door and ridge of the roof are aligned down slope, while most bank barns are aligned with ridge along the hill. The stable (for oxen, horses, mules, livestock) and main entrance are, by custom and logic when possible, arranged to face south or southeast for best protection from weather and maximum light inside. Walls are eighteen inches thick; outside dimensions are 32 x 68' with a 12' threshing floor. An 1840s hand-forged strap hinge (2" x 35") on new plank door; while these hinges are a pattern used by German builders, they are found on barns built by Anglo-Americans as well. The 10" x 12" broadaxe-hewn summer beam supports elaborately joined and pegged timbers under the hayloft. (2003)

(Photos Above) A. F. Brinkmann farm, near Mount Sterling. The stone barn and house were built for Brinkmann, the son of Francis William (F. W.) and Wilhelmina C. Gehner Brinkmann. F. W. Brinkmann was born in Prussia in 1820 and came to the United States about 1849. This *bank barn* is similar in form and construction to Linneman and others in the area, yet it has its own layout. The banked portion is uphill, with a gable door leading to a granary. The jamb of the rear doorwall is enscribed with "1874."[6] The framework inside and roof system are heavy frame construction with mortise and tenon construction. Superb details include hand-forged hardware and "Dutch" or "double" barn doors. (Middle Left) Threshing floor and front door.

(Left) A. F. Brinkmann *log double-crib barn* of hewn oak timbers with corners V-notched, a style typically used by Anglo-American pioneers as well as German-Americans. Feed mangers are hollowed-out logs under racks of split-oak sticks to hold hay pitched down from the loft. An important detail is the construction of the gables, with vertical riven studs supporting horizontal riven boards (often taken to be a German building trait). Such marvelous evidence of the ingenuity and skill of the pioneer builder are usually demolished or replaced. (2003)

This fine Morgan County barn illustrates two features prominent on some bank barns—the pent roof and the purpose-built ramp. In places where the prairie terrain was relentlessly flat, they nevertheless had their banks, produced by mounding up earth or by constructing a wooden bridge to reach the main door. The *pent roof* or *canopy* is a feature rooted in British and German barns, and a common feature on so-called *Pennsylvania barns*. The pent roof is a small shed roof attached to provide additional shelter for livestock. They are usually unsupported by posts. Some are small, others large enough to shelter a wagon.

(Right) In Morgan County, far from the core of the Missouri Rhineland, are *bank barns* built by Swiss Mennonite farmers who came after the Civil War. These barns seem to have all the elements of a so-called *Pennsylvania barn* type except an unsupported *forebay*. (1948, Historic American Buildings Survey, Library of Congress)

(Photos Left and Below) In southern Moniteau County, Louis Bruce built in limestone. A miller, Bruce came from Virginia in 1858 and developed Rock Enon Farm. The 1860 census noted two stone masons living nearby, Anglo-American if we judge by names, John Parcrust and L. B. Moore, as well as a stone mason named George Goeble, a Germanic name. The bank barn has a date stone reading "L. B. 1870." The barn defies easy analysis due to lack of a large front door to accompany farming activities; there is no evidence of the barn used to store farm produce. The farm is on the National Register of Historic Places.[7] The house is an *I-house*, the favored type among most Anglo-Americans, and eventually many German immigrants as well. The 180-foot-long retaining wall, dated 1873, is among the finest stone walls in Missouri. (Below Right) Bank barn, 70' x 50'. (Below) Farm plan. (Photos and drawing by Deb Sheals 1991, courtesy Historic Preservation Program, Missouri Department of Natural Resources)

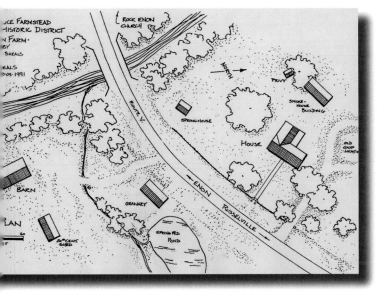

The *bank barn* sometimes has doors on the gable ends rather than the sides. These are not common in Missouri. Builders paid strict attention to the advantages of the site's contour, and a very strong preference for hillside sites can be seen. In places such as the north Missouri prairies, where the topography was flat, builders continued the basement tradition by molding a mound of dirt into a ramp up to the main floor. The large door and entrance for the wagon and equipment made access easy.

(Top Photo) The Edmund Hosmer farm near Marshfield (Webster County) represents the evolution of the dairy industry. Hosmer came from Massachusetts in 1871 where his father's farm was next to Ralph Waldo Emerson's. Henry David Thoreau included "Farmer Hosmer" in his *Men of Concord*. Edmund Hosmer's four-hundred-acre farm in Missouri led in developing dairying, which he began after study of the potential of his "poor Ozark soil."[8] Hosmer built new barns around 1900. His dairy barn had room for one hundred milk cows, all milked by hand. So many hired hands stayed at the farm that it became known as "Hosmer town." Hosmer is said to have installed the first silo in Webster County in 1908, and he brought in the first cream separator, manure spreader, hay loader, gasoline engine, and other new machines. Sweet butter from Hosmer's Jersey cows sold across the Ozarks and in markets as distant as St. Louis. Webster County became known as one of the top dairy counties in the United States. In the 1920s, the Hosmers went into the tomato industry—an important but brief part of the Ozarks' economic history. Hosmer's farm exemplified the growing commercialism of farming and sales to city people. His new barns included a dairy barn incorporating the bank barn concept, with entry in the gable. (Photo by Cathy Brown 1995, courtesy Historic Preservation Program, Missouri Department of Natural Resources)

(Left and Bottom Photos) Bank barns were built well into the twentieth century. The Kemp milk barn in Andrew County from the late 1930s is a two-level bank barn on flat ground with an earthen ramp to the main floor. The framing is an impressive web of oak lumber secured with nails and braces. (Photos by Travis W. Gallup 2003)

Design 2557—For 16 Cows and 5 Horses

Price of Complete working plans and specifications for Design 2557 $5.00

(Above) Companies like the Louden Company sold plans for bank barns, as in this 1915 catalog.

(Top Right) Bank barn with ramp in the gable, near LaPlata. (Macon County 1974)

(Right) Among the best-known bank barns is the enormous barn at Huber's Ferry on the bluffs overlooking the Osage and Maries Rivers on U.S. 50 in eastern Osage County. (Photo by Jim McCarty 2003)

(Bottom Two Photos) Bank barns were recorded in a survey by Roger Maserang along the Johnson County–Lafayette County border. Maserang's work was accomplished with a regional planning commission, an important kind of institution for the future of Missouri's historic buildings and landscapes. (Bottom Left) McCurdy barn, Johnson County circa 1900, horizontal siding with opening in gable end. (Bottom Right) This example in southern Lafayette County is the more familiar form, a frame barn built atop stone basement walls with a ramp entrance. (Photos by Roger Maserang 1986, courtesy Historic Preservation Program, Missouri Department of Natural Resources)

(Left) In Maserang's survey in Johnson County there appeared an unusual bank barn, the Amos Markey barn from the late nineteenth century. It has a forebay which is unsupported. This feature typically marks a bank barn as a Pennsylvania barn type. The entire barn is handsomely made of timber frame construction of a high caliber. (Roger Maserang)

(Photo Above and Left) The Oakes bank barn, Newton County, documented for MoDOT, offers another variation. From the front it seems a typical bank barn. From the rear its added space, projecting much as a forebay, provided additional hay storage. (Courtesy Cultural Resources, Missouri Department of Transportation)

(Above) One of the important buildings surveyed for MoDOT in 1993 prior to highway improvement decisions was the Louis Sohn barn near Lee's Summit, Jackson County, established by Mathius Speed in 1844 near the wagon road to Blue Springs. Louis Sohn bought the place in 1873 and the barn was built in 1916. According to family history, Sohn hired a crew of some fifteen Germans supervised by a ship's carpenter to design and construct the building. The job took eight months and cost $3,000,[9] and the barn exhibits outstanding timber frame construction, with framework from oak timber on Sohn's farm. Arkansas pine lumber for the weatherboarding was purchased from Long Lumber in Grandview. The structure was laid out as a hay and alfalfa barn with a capacity of 80 tons of loose hay. The basement housed six teams of draft horses and several dairy cows. By the 1950s, the last team of draft horses was replaced by machines, and hogs began to be housed in the basement. (1993, Jackson County) The chevron-shaped diagonal weatherboarding is rare. Destroyed in 1976 during construction of Interstate 470. (Courtesy Robert J. Reeder, Cultural Resources, Missouri Department of Transportation)

One of North America's most photogenic and admired barns is the *Pennsylvania barn*. This barn type, while exhibiting Continental influences, is "American." The *Pennsylvania barn* was frequently vast and well constructed and built by English farmers alongside German farmers. These barns have become famous. Justly so. The genesis of this barn type seems to be German-speaking immigrants who came to Pennsylvania, Maryland, and Virginia in the late seventeenth and early eighteenth centuries.[10] This barn type is generally larger than the British-based three-bay barns. It includes spaces for animals as well as the threshing and storing of crops. The Pennsylvania barn from the front closely resembles many "English" type barns—one large building with a large door in the center. Like many bank barns in America, it has a lower level (usually called a "basement" and usually built of stone) where livestock are stabled.

In every element except one, the *Pennsylvania barn* is a two-level three-bay *bank barn* with a central ramp to the threshing floor and grain and hay storage areas. The feature that seems to justify definition as a separate type is the projecting main floor (*forebay*) that extends out over the basement stables, and is not supported by posts or walls. The forebay added protection for the livestock and stabling area below. To many scholars, the forebay on a bank barn defines the type, whether or not the farmers came from Pennsylvania or Ohio, Switzerland or Germany. Using only one feature—the cantilevered forebay—to define a separate barn type seems narrow.

Thanks to Tom Carneal's field survey in the early 1980s, we have at least one documented *Pennsylvania barn* that might satisfy the scholars' definition. Splendid in its clarity and quality, the Ozenberger barn was built in Buchanan County, a few miles east of St. Joe, in 1847 by four German-speaking Swiss immigrants. The four Ozenberger brothers were part of a group of Swiss who first came to Holmes County, Ohio, in 1831, and then to northwest Missouri in 1847; Jacob moved on to Kansas, while Nicholas, Frederick and Peter settled in Buchanan County and set up farming.[11] It is worth emphasizing that Buchanan County is quite distant from the "Rhineland" region of German settlement where so much research has been done.[12]

(Above) Ozenberger barn, Buchanan County, was an exceptionally rare and important example of a form of bank barn with unsupported forebay. Destroyed by fire in 1995. (Courtesy Tom Carneal)

And how interesting that the Ozenberger barn was built by Swiss immigrants, the group most suggested in the scholarship as the people bringing this type of barn to America.

A European Housebarn in the Upper Ozarks

(Above) William Pelster and his third wife, Rebekah Kreutzer, with stepchildren, circa 1900. (Courtesy Alfred Pelster 1982)

We come now to what is perhaps Missouri's most famous barn, unique in its functions and a barn with a fascinating biography—the Pelster "housebarn," dating from circa 1855. The added interest of *Fachwerk* construction of a high order and retention of original 1860s fabric makes the Pelster family's housebarn a world-class historic site.[13]

In the pressure of assimilation, many immigrants put aside old systems of thinking. Yet manifestations of Old World thinking endure. The William Pelster housebarn is a structure housing animals, agricultural activities, the produce and equipment of the harvest and members of the family in a single, complex building. A housebarn here can be seen as a creative response by an individual farmer with a deep sense of conservatism to the basic needs for shelter. And it can remind us that many immigrants found purpose and pleasure in reinstalling certain of the old European patterns of living that most others had forsaken.

Although other *housebarns*—*Einhaus* and *Wollstallhaus* are the closest words in German—may well have been built in Missouri, we believe this is the only one that survives, although, interestingly, there is a revival of the tradition among some present-day Amish families that have built longhouses with space for family, work, and horses. A dozen or so old housebarns have survived in German-speaking communities in the Midwest, Great Plains, and Canada. Documented examples survive in Wisconsin, Minnesota, North Dakota, South Dakota, Nebraska, Kansas, and Texas, in addition to Missouri's one example.

The concept of a single unit housing people and animals as well as crops is widespread across all of Europe and the British Isles. There are many varieties there, from the small *longhouse* of several rooms side by side in Celtic Britain to the huge, broad *Hallenhaus* of the Low Countries to the multistoried examples in Alpine environments to the south and into northern Italy.

But the advantages of the single unit did not pertain to the American experience. Here, there was plenty of space for a variety of buildings on one's farm, quite different from the small and controlled spaces of the Old World. In America the zest for land and expansion took over, and people were able to spread out to establish a farm that was separate, large, and private. The tightly arranged old European farmstead generally faded from use.

Friedrich Wilhelm Pelster (1825–1908) was a self-reliant *plattdeutsch* Lutheran farmer in Franklin County. He came to America in 1842 at age seventeen with his parents from the village of Dissen, near Osnabruck, Hanover. The Pelster farm was located some ten miles south of the Missouri River in an area often called "the new Germania." As with numerous German-speaking farms, the farmstead is located away from the main road. The site itself is on mid-slope, well above the bottom land and below the woods along the hills. On this site, Pelster banked his barn just as many others with sloping land did. While this geographic place technically is in the upper or "border" of the Ozarks, this is a very German community tied to similar rural communities west and east of it.

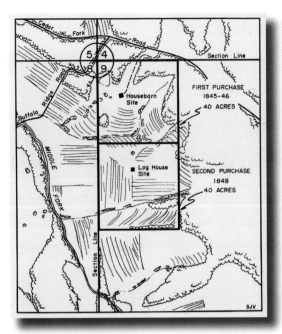

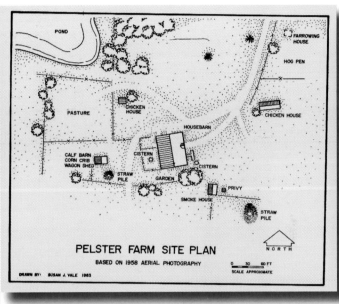

(Above Left) Landscape of the Pelster farm (drawing by Susan J. Vale). (Above Right) Pelster farmsite plan. (Susan J. Vale)

(Bottom Right) Plan of main floor: "house," central threshing floor (*Diele* in Missouri German usage), granaries, and storerooms. Overall dimensions are 62' x 54'. (Plan by Susan J. Vale 1983)

The left or south third became the dwelling, with a cellar below. As a result, some people in the area call it "the Pelster house," while others call it "the Pelster barn." The term *housebarn* is used mostly by outsiders. The Pelster family, according to Alfred Pelster in 1983, had no *plattdeutsch* word for "housebarn," but offered *hausstahl*—"house and stall." They tended to call the building a "house," but Mr. Pelster remembered that his grandfather (the builder) did have a German term for the building, which had been lost from oral tradition through the years.

Some have said the layout of the Pelster housebarn is most like examples in middle or southwestern Germany. However, its *Fachwerk* (half-timbering) seems more like construction traditions in northern Germany, where the Pelster family came from.

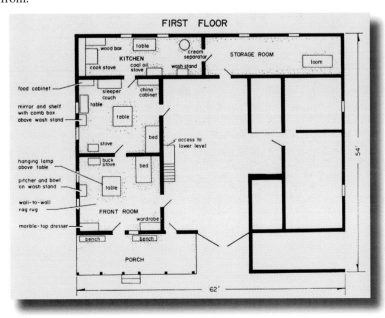

(Left) Heavy timber framed walls of "front room", the other side of this wall does not have limestone nogging. This wall faces the threshing floor, the stairway goes to upstairs sleeping rooms. (Top Right) Mortise and tenon joint. The four slash marks are the carpenter's Roman numerals that indicate where this horizontal timber is to fit into the vertical timber. (Bottom Right) Rear wall of threshing floor: *Fachwerk* with "cotton rock" nogging used in this area among German builders of the first generation. (1983)

In 1983, Alfred Pelster solved the unanswered riddle of sources for the housebarn. The original Pelster family farm, several miles east, was laid out by Wilhelm Pelster's father, Phillip, in the early 1840s when they came from Osnabruck. At this time, Wilhelm was a young man, and helped with the construction of the home place. At this important farm east of the Pelster housebarn, there is the splendid *Fachwerk* house using the same construction methods that William (Wilhelm) used some twenty years later when he married and built the housebarn on his own farm.

(Right) Pelster home place in 1983. (Below) Site plan by S. Vale. (Middle) *Fachwerk* house built by Philip Pelster circa 1844. (Bottom) 66' x 41' V-notched log double-crib barn; its spatial organization was utilized later by Philip's son William in the housebarn.

Also on the home place, there is a log double-crib barn, which served as the model for the spatial arrangement of the housebarn young Pelster would build. Pelster pulled together the half-timbering construction method (remembered from Germany and a strong tradition in his area in Franklin County) with the three-bay barn concept (seen in many log double-crib barns here), set it up as a bank barn, and added space for his family. Since there are no exact models or parallels known back in Germany, this seems a reasonable explanation to the interesting question, "Why a housebarn?"

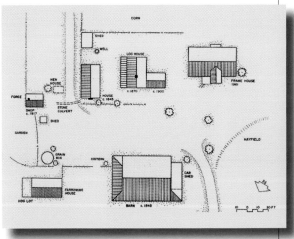

Housebarn circa 1982 and 1989 after a protective coat of whi base paint was applied (originally the building was yellow). (Left) Visitors are part of a tour of German Missouri sites for members of the Vernacular Architecture Forum hosted by Osmund Overby and Howard Marshall. (1989)

While this building speaks of Germany, it is thoroughly American as well. While Mr. Pelster logically built a traditional central threshing floor, it seems that it was never used, due to new threshing techniques and machinery. Pelster was innovative in his use of the latest farm equipment. He had the first corn binder and first sheet metal roof in Franklin County (laid over the 1850s wooden shingles). Pelster chose modern double-hung sash windows rather than casement windows that had become old-fashioned. We may suggest that the Pelster housebarn symbolizes the combination of the Old World traditions blending together with Missouri ideas in this interesting second-generation farm.

The process of figuring out how to build a house or a barn is not a simple one. For this farmer, William Pelster, his affection for his German roots and family led to a distinctly unusual decision to design and construct a housebarn. The place of the Pelster building is important in Missouri history. Its story attests both the creativity and to the strength of traditions. As an object, the building suggests the ultimate construction on the Missouri frontier of an Old World building type quickly replaced in the American experience. As an image, the building has symbolic power for Missourians who appreciate it as a product of craftsmanship of world-class quality.

This is a well-known historic site, appearing in van Ravenswaay's epic 1977 book. The property became part of the Missouri State Parks system and is on the National Register. The future of the site seems safe and it is expected that, when state government resources become available, the Pelster housebarn will become part of a series of historic sites that speak of Missouri's complex German-speaking heritage.

(Below) The Pelster family and building were featured in an exhibition developed by Barry Bergey and the author at University of Missouri-Columbia in 1983 to mark the tricentennial of German immigration to America. The young man with the violin is Reinhart Poppelmeyer, who joined the Army in World War I and was killed in battle in Europe. (Family album photos courtesy Alfred Pelster)

THE TRANSVERSE-CRIB BARN

7

A new kind of barn type emerged at the end of the eighteenth century in the upper South and took root on the Missouri landscape, brought by farmers from the Kentucky Bluegrass and Tennessee Valley. The *transverse-crib barn* is among the few barn forms developed in the United States. It evolved from the English barn.

By the time the Midwest was settled, the standard frame barn of the Ohio or Missouri farm family dwarfed most of the barns of the Old World. Often, the erection of a particularly vast or handsome barn—such as the costly and beautiful red brick barns of the Midwest—was a signal to neighbors and visitors that the owner had reached the pinnacle of economic success.

The majority of early barns had main doors along the side. In the *transverse-crib barn*, its defining feature is the shift of the main door from the side to the gable end. This shift can be seen in older barns in the Southeast, and particularly in piedmont and bluegrass regions of Virginia, North Carolina, Kentucky, and Tennessee. This barn type became a familiar form throughout our state because of its great flexibility and relative ease in design and construction. There is plenty of space for everything—horse stalls, livestock feeding bunks, interior granaries, storage areas for tractors and farm equipment, and that vast hayloft where loose hay could be loaded.

(Above) John Gammon's transverse-crib barn east of Walker was new around 1910 (Vernon County). Left to right are Aline Charles, Neil Charles and (in buggy) Virginia Gammon. The barn was built by Elijah W. Ransdell, Mrs. Gammon's grandfather. He was a carpenter who built houses, barns, and churches, as well as helping build the Vernon County Courthouse. They painted the barn red with white trim. (Courtesy Knox McCrory)

(Left) Transverse-crib barn in Boone County (Ellis), from 1870s county history; the Ellis farm includes a log double-crib barn and Anglo-American type I house. Loading hay with block and tackle near Eagleville, Harrison County, 1950s, in the period when loose hay was losing out to square bales. (Photo by Gerald Massie, Missouri Division of Commerce and Industrial Development; courtesy Missouri State Archives)

(Right) At White Haven, the Frederick Dent farm in south St. Louis County, the barn was recorded in the Historic American Buildings Survey in 1940; U. S. Grant married Dent's daughter and owned the property for a time.

By the twentieth century the *transverse-crib* and the *English barn* forms (including the bank barn) became Missouri's most significant and common ones. In some regions of the state, the transverse-crib barn replaced other barn types almost completely, as in the Ozarks and Little Dixie. Its flexibility and practicality meant that its plan was featured in many builder's manuals and farm journals, dressed in the latest technology and innovations.

(Above) The timber framed barn at the Daniel Boone historic site in St. Charles County was dated to 1850 through dendrochronology (tree-ring dating). (2003)

(Left) The "Tom Hodge place," a typical Little Dixie barn on old Anglo-American farms. (Boone County) (Middle Left) Bill Creson's timber-frame barn in Howard County was built by his grandfather, who came from North Carolina in about 1850. (Bottom Left) Ralls County 2003. (Below) Stoddard County. (Ryan Mooney)

(Top) Warren County. (Above) Cape Girardeau County.
(Above, Right) Callaway County. (Right) Bollinger County.
(Below Right) Cooper County (2003).

The early Anglo-American farmers from Kentucky, Tennessee, and other upland states were so important in establishing this barn type in Missouri that the transverse-crib barn became a key ingredient in defining a large cultural region of central and northeast Missouri as "Little Dixie."[1] The barn is easily expandable on all sides. Often, the gable end was furnished with an additional passage by bringing the gable forward or by adding a shed addition across the front. This space allows shelter for wagons and equipment.

In the evolution of the *transverse-crib barn* in the upper South, the *log four-crib barn* appears, but rarely. Log four-crib barns were built in earlier times, but the form was abandoned as the transverse-crib took over. The four-crib barn is a transitional form of barn between the English barn and log double-crib and the transverse crib barn. In a sense, this four-crib barn is two English barn types (one bay deep) built next to each other, with a gable roof covering everything including a broad hallway down the middle.

Four-crib barns: (Left) In this Reynolds County four-crib log barn provided by Lynn Morrow of the Missouri State Archives, logs are hewn flat with a broadaxe and corners are held together, without nails, in the half-dovetail cornering method that is one of Missouri's two main corner-timbering methods (the other is V-notching); near Ellington; this important building has been lost. (1983)

Many fine examples of the transverse-crib type may be found across Missouri. In Johnson County, the old Fulkerson barn was built around 1912. (Top Two Photos) Fulkerson barn, Johnson County 1985. (Photos by Roger Maserang, courtesy Historic Preservation Program, Missouri Department of Natural Resources).

(Right) In southern Randolph County, the Perkins place has a large mid-1900s general-purpose barn. Framing lumber is circle-sawn oak, and mortise and tenon joints secure the most vital posts, beams, and braces. A generation earlier, these major posts would probably have been hand hewn instead of sawn. It was standard practice to use sawn lumber, but retain the age-old mortise and tenon methods from the time of local sawmills and lumberyards well into the twentieth century. The large beams are crucial to structural integrity and the best method of securing them until recently was the mortise and tenon pegged joint. The barn was covered with sheet metal to protect the aging weatherboarding. (Bottom) Mortise and tenon joinery; oak pegs protrude slightly through the mortise (hole) for hanging things up. (2003)

Wight barn, sixty by seventy-eight feet, in Randolph County, circa 1900. On the other side of Randolph County in the Milton community, the Wight transverse-crib barn replaced older barns around 1900. At that time, the gambrel roof was becoming desirable for its added loft space. James F. R. Wight was the son of a Scottish immigrant cabinetmaker named James Wight who left the eastern Scottish Lowlands for Virginia in 1794 and then moved across the Blue Ridge to Kentucky. In about 1838 he led a wagon train from Shelby County, Kentucky and established a tobacco, horse, and mule farm called Wightland.[2] (Top Two Photos) Barn in 1972, barn in 2003. (Left) Hayloft with gambrel roof trusses.

Across the road, at the author's home place, Wight gave half the farm to his daughter Frances, who married Moberly banker John B. Jennings. Their daughter Frances Jennings married Charles W. Marshall, and they developed the farm around champion Hereford cattle in the 1940s and 1950s. This farm had been where the farm manager lived before the Civil War and was called Locust Grove Farm. (Bottom) Transverse-crib barn from the 1850s with cross-passage on the north gable, 1973; plan.

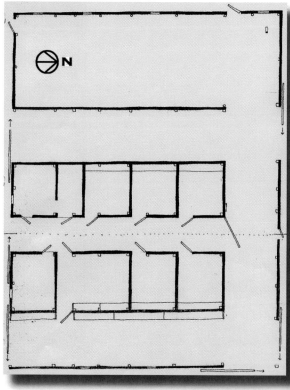

(Above) The form is suitable for dairy barns. The hallway down the middle is logical, dividing rows of milking stanchions. Such barns may be large, since more room can be added to gable ends. At the Longwell farm in Livingston County, the Southern-type farmhouse is surrounded by modern barns with gambrel roofs that replaced earlier barns. The barns, silo, and cattle-handling arrangement is elaborate and impressive. The milk barn has walls of ceramic block, in keeping with emerging regulations and standards for milk production in the early twentieth century. (Photo by Jim McCarty 2002)

(Two Midde Photos) Businessman J. C. Penney was from Caldwell County and as success came to him he developed farms in the Hamilton area where various advanced agricultural practices were carried out. Aerial view of Penney's farm near Hamilton, and the Penney-James farm, where the barn walls were entirely ceramic block. (Photos by Gerald Massie, 1950s, courtesy Missouri State Archives)

(Bottom) Ralph Richterkessing farm in 1991, barn, and farm plan. In St. Charles County, expansion of the St. Louis metropolitan area and highways rubs out countless farmsteads. Two of these farms have been recorded by cultural resources staff of the Missouri Department of Transportation in Jefferson City. The Richterkessing farms contained important buildings and reflected German immigration in the early nineteenth century in St. Louis and St. Charles Counties. The Meyer and Richterkessing families came from the Hanover region of northern Germany in the 1860s.[3] (Courtesy Cultural Resources, Missouri Department of Transportation, Jefferson City)

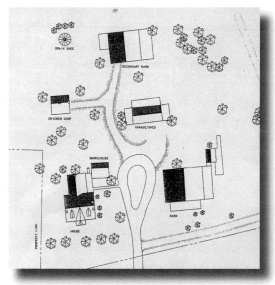

Transverse-crib barns in Texas County. Like north of the Missouri River, the transverse-crib barn is the definitive barn type for the interior Ozarks, including the Arkansas Ozarks. (Top and Middle Left) Jim Kidwell's gambrel-roof barn, built in the 1920s, near Yukon; Kidwell with Katahdin sheep. (Bottom) McCubbin's frame barn circa 1890, hewn sills and floor system, remainder of lumber circle-sawn yellow pine; vertical interior posts are skinned poles. Note the owl hole in a diamond pattern in the gable. (2003)

(Top) In Howell County near Pomona, Sim Goyer's barn, built in 1893 of red oak. (Courtesy of Cliff Bryan 2003)

(Right) Small transverse-crib barns often are surrounded by sheds for equipment storage and livestock feeding. Bryant farm, Andrew County. (Photo by Travis W. Gallup 2003)

People find new uses for barns and take pride in them. (Top) Flag barn, Marceline. (Linn County, photo by Travis W. Gallup 2003). (Left) Antique shop, Bollinger County. (Bottom) Children's store, Jackson (Cape Girardeau County). (2003)

Walt Disney (1901–1966), one of Missouri's illustrious native sons, based much of his work on his recollections of growing up in Marceline. His backyard railroad shop in Los Angeles was constructed in 1950 to resemble the way he remembered the red frame transverse-crib barn at his parent's small farm near Marceline. The California replica was his "happy place" where imagination flowered, and was headquarters for his miniature steam train. The Missouri barn was destroyed years ago, but Disney fondly recalled it as the stage for his youthful experiments with drama and shows he called his "barn circus." Admission, ten cents.[4] In 2001, the centennial of Disney's birth, a replica of "the California barn" was erected in Marceline. Called "the Missouri barn," the replica of Disney's California railroad shop recalls real Missouri hay barns of the nineteenth century.

(Top) Walt Disney's "California barn" in Los Angeles, California, 1950. It was moved to Griffith Park and is open to visitors. (Photo by Michael Broggie) (Bottom) The replica of Disney's California barn was built in Marceline in 2001. (Photo by Scott Rule)

BARNS FOR TOBACCO, BARNS FOR MULES

Among the specialized barns in Missouri are tobacco barns, a uniquely-American kind of barn. Tobacco is harvested green and must be cured in a shelter before shipping to the market. Tobacco culture is labor intensive and demanding and tobacco-growing in Missouri depended in large part upon slave labor before the Civil War and Emancipation. A good income could be derived from a relatively small acreage if the soil was correct, well graded and the product handled.

SCHUYLER

The French colonial farmers grew tobacco, using it for "snuff taking" rather than smoking, while the Spanish in colonial times introduced cigar smoking (importing their leaf from Cuba and Louisiana). Members of the Lewis and Clark expedition up the Missouri River in 1804–1806 took tobacco with them, and when their supplies ran out the smokers are said to have resorted to the inner bark of red willow and the chewers to wild crab tree bark.[5]

After the Louisiana Purchase (1804), Kentucky, Tennessee, and Virginia farmers brought tobacco plants and seed with them by horseback and mover wagon. In the

(Above) In 1904, tobacco was still a significant crop north in Schuyler County, along the Iowa border, as this field and fine barn prove. (Williams, *State of Missouri*)

1820s, tobacco was being grown in Howard, Chariton, Boone, and other central Missouri counties on the Missouri River and was shipped down from market ports such as Glasgow and Rocheport. Tobacco was being grown along the Mississippi River, too, especially in Pike and Ralls Counties. Practically every village along the Missouri River had a tobacco wharf and warehouse. Tobacco was grown in many parts of early Missouri, including counties like St. Charles, Lincoln, and Warren.[6] Eventually, planting and processing developed most thoroughly along the Missouri River (especially north of the river) from Callaway County west and north to Buchanan County.

(Left) J. R. Hickam's tobacco barn, with Mr. Hickam. This Irish-American family raised white burley above the Missouri River for several generations. (Above) Interior with rails. (Bottom Left) A hay barn converted to tobacco curing; the long-unused silo sports a hackberry tree. (Moniteau County 2003)

(Top) W. O. Hickam's tobacco barn on Splice Creek, Moniteau County. The roof projects forward to shelter a cross-passage in front of the main doors. (Bottom Right) Inside is a forest of *rails* for hanging tobacco; tobacco is no longer raised, so the rails serve other purposes, such as hanging up some home-cured hams. (Above) Current owner Gerald Stevens, and grandson Josey. (2003).

(Above) L-R: J. R. Hickam (son of the builder), Josey, grandson of current owner Gerald Stevens. (2003)

Tobacco and hemp used to make ropes became the most significant cash crops in Missouri in its early years. For a time, St. Louis led the nation in tobacco production. Not coincidentally Missouri is still the leading producer of corncob pipes, an industry all but single-handedly created in the mid-nineteenth century by Henry Tibbe in Washington (Franklin County), supplying the world, and such famous corncob pipe enthusiasts as the legendary General Douglas McArthur, with "Missouri meerschaums."[7]

In 1945, J. R. Hickam hired his uncle Lonnie Hickam and a friend, Ralph Stock, to build this tobacco barn on his farm in Moniteau County. Measuring thirty-six feet across by forty feet deep, and sixteen feet tall, the large doors on both ends provide easy access for the wagon bringing in the harvested leaves for curing. On the south side, Hickam built a lean-to addition where he fed cattle. Tall narrow louvered doors on the north side of the barn are opened to let the natural forces of air mature the leaves. At night the doors are shut and the barn sealed up tightly to try to keep moisture out. Many tobacco barns have large doors on both ends that can be opened completely during the daytime. Mr. Hickam's father, the late W. O. Hickam (a well-known fiddle player as well as a tobacco farmer), built a new tobacco barn in 1946 that could hold six *rails* of tobacco on sticks. The barn is aligned with the other farm buildings along the brow of the hill facing south and the tobacco field below. A gambrel roof offers

additional space for the highest rail and, with the roof extended forward, a hayloft is located in the cross-passage driveway. If necessary in abundant crop years, the hayloft was also loaded with tobacco. It took thousands of tobacco sticks to hold a whole crop.

Tobacco was sometimes air cured and the process was completed by the firing method, in which artificial heat added value to the leaves when marketed. Tobacco farmers use different kinds of presses to help compress the cured leaves in bundles on the sticks. A tobacco press is typically attached to the wall of the *stripping room* or *shed*. The stripping room or shed is furnished with a stove so the workers can be comfortable when stripping and pressing is accomplished in the winter. Many farmers then hauled the bales of pressed and dried leaves to the Weston tobacco market.

Bundles were shipped in bales of circa seventy-five pounds to market in late winter, and from there were shipped to St. Louis and New Orleans. In former times, tobacco was shipped in wooden barrels called "hogsheads" (typically 54" x 40" wide at the head).

While many tobacco barns generally take the *transverse-crib* plan, some were built as bank barns due to the slope of the farmer's property.

Barns for drying tobacco are also found in the northwest part of the state, where soils and climate favor the crop. In Buchanan County, for example, Tom Carneal's fine survey of historic sites documented an example in the St. Joseph area. A *transverse-crib* type barn, it has the familiar louvered doors along the sides for air circulation.

(Top) Tobacco barn at Wooldridge (Cooper County) appears to have been converted from a *bank barn*. (2003).

(Above) At the Everett Jacobs farm near Huntsdale in the hills near the Missouri River in western Boone County (one of the few places tobacco is still grown), two barns were used for curing. The farm was established in the 1850s by W. T. Jacobs from Shelby County, Kentucky.[8] In the 1970s, six acres of tobacco were grown, which the government translated into a quota of sixty-three hundred pounds. One of these barns is a transverse-crib barn with a large gambrel roof that served double duty as a hay barn and tobacco barn. The hayloft was fitted out with the network of crossed poles that allow the tobacco to be hung up on the sticks and air cured. Such practical alterations of existing barns help us understand the scarcity of purpose-built tobacco barns. (1974)

(Bottom Two Photos) Behind that barn is a barn Jacobs designed specifically for air-curing tobacco. This frame barn, taking the transverse-crib plan, is some thirty-six feet wide by ninety-four feet long, with a gable roof. Inside there are small rooms in each end for tobacco equipment and maintenance, the north room as the stripping room. Barn and stripping room in 1974. (2003)

While we have tremendous work and pleasure horses in our state, we are particularly well-known for mules. There are few symbols as powerful to Missourians. The space suitable for draft horses was suitable for mules, but with stall doors higher than horse stall doors. Mules can, and will, jump over stall doors of average height. A mule barn used on the regular family farm, however, differed only slightly from other general-purpose barns that sheltered livestock, machinery, work animals, and crops. The feed rack for mules was frequently positioned at head height so mules would feed with their heads up to encourage stylish head carriage. And more than one farmer has added a new and heavier sill or wall section to replace one that has been damaged by being kicked by a bored or insulted mule.

(Top) Jones tobacco barn, near Rushville (Buchanan County 1981). (Courtesy Tom Carneal)

(Right) President Harry S Truman and mules at the Missouri State Fair. (Private collection)

(Bottom) Threshing at the State Prison Farm near Jefferson City in the 1950s. (Photo by Gerald Massie)

Mule breeders with the resources often constructed elaborate, even palatial, barns for their stock.

(Above) Brick mule barn near Louisiana (Pike County 1974).

(Left) Leonard estate, "Ravenswood," Cooper County (Historic American Buildings Survey).

(Top) P. Smith farm, Boone County, illustrated in 1875 (Edwards) with special Mule Barn and mule lot.

(Above) Mule barn built 1891–92 for a prominent Scotch-Irish farmer and businessman in northwest Missouri, David Rankin, at Tarkio (Atchison County).

(Right) Rebuilt after the 1908 fire; three-story red brick barn built with eight sides. Destroyed by an additional fire several years ago. (Courtesy Missouri State Archives)

(Left) In Randolph County, Green Wilcox and Renick carpenter Roy Vance built Wilcox's new mule barn for $5,000 in 1921–22. They used white and red oak sawn from Thrasher's Mill east of Moberly. Designed as a mule-breeding barn, with hayloft, it featured the same kind of clerestory windows as several other barns in this area. Green's son Bob and grandson Wayne plan to cover the front and rear with sheet metal. (2003)

Most nineteenth century mules were black with white points, but breeders eventually discovered that the Belgian draft horse mare could produce mule foals that were easier to match into teams that were physically alike, attractive, and of uniform color, and this mule breed and color led to today's light blond "sorrel mule."

In its heyday, from the Civil War to around 1910, the mule was the dominant work animal in many regions of the United States. The mule was the foundation of commerce in Missouri, the state that brought it to its highest point in development. Missouri mules hauled tons of freight and people in the Westward Movement, moved military supplies, and cultivated cotton. Once famous for their mules, Missourians are rediscovering the importance of the animal. The draft mule show at the Missouri State Fair is one of the largest in the world. Jumping mules are popular in shows and coon hunters and mules still work Missouri forests and farmlands.[9]

(Above) One of the well-known mules from this neighborhood was "Missouri Queen," posed in front of the newspaper office in Moberly. Wilcox's partner, mule dealer Midge Marshall showed this mule at state fairs in Missouri, Iowa, and Illinois in 1905, winning first prize in each event. (Courtesy Bob Wilcox)

Mules figured prominently in the Civil War, hauling and helping both Union and Confederate causes. Missouri provided thousands of mules to the Army during the Spanish-American War of 1898 and to the British in the Boer War of 1901–1902. Missouri mules rose to international prominence during the muddy trench campaigns in Europe in World War I. In 1914, Guyton and Harrington established trade with the government of Great Britain to supply horses and mules for military use against the Germans in Europe, thereby becoming the leading international supplier for World War I.

When general-purpose tractors were perfected by manufacturers in the mid-1920s, farmers took up the new technology. A tractor replaced two and a half mules or draft horses. By the 1940s, the market for draft horses and mules plunged. The mule became rare, a family pet rather than the engine of agricultural commerce. Apart from the occasional logger or small farmer, and among some Amish and Mennonite farmers, the mule's fieldwork is done.

MR. BRADLEY'S NEW CATTLE BARN

After World War II, Aubrey and Thelma Bradley decided to build a new place. They had lived and farmed a few miles northeast, near the original Bradley family home place. With improved economic times, the Bradleys bought the old Adams farm and hired the Boswell brothers to construct a barn and brick house. Walter and Robert Boswell were well-known barn builders and house carpenters in Randolph County and part of a farm family in the area.

(Right) Bradley barn south of Huntsville, Randolph County. (Photo by John D. Marshall 2003)

(Below) Aerial photo from the 1950s; Orb and Thelma laid out their new house and barn aligned and set back from the gravel road to the east; the brick house was built by "the Boswell boys" in 1953, two years after completing the barn. (Courtesy Dorothy Ann and Lemuel Robb)

The new barn was begun in 1949 and completed in 1951. The Boswell brothers served as the foremen and lead carpenters, with a crew of four young men, including William Lemuel Robb (who married Mr. Bradley's daughter Dorothy Ann), Vernice Ransdell, Robert Oliver, and Press Oliver. Lemuel Robb well remembers the hard work of being on the carpenter crew. Hand tools were used for everything once the timbers and boards came from the mill. Mr. Bradley bought forty acres of old growth white oak several miles south of the site, and sawmill operator E. H. Thrasher brought his mill and set it up at the forty-acres. Thrasher sawed out the lumber and posts, and the construction crew hauled the material to the barn site on Mr. Bradley's farm trucks.

In its plan, measuring some 128 feet wide by 180 feet in length, this new barn took the horizontal layout of older transverse-crib general purpose barns in the area. In fact, this is one of the last large general purpose barns to be built, because these were the years when many farmers were changing to prefabricated pole barns and machine sheds set up for specific purposes. There is a fourteen-foot-wide drive down the middle from gable to gable.

Mr. Bradley designed the barn to echo a big new barn built by his friend and neighbor, Henderson Wilcox, as well as to reflect the design of several other barns in this neighborhood of southern Randolph County.

The roof design is called a "monitor roof" and is used in large-span structures such as factory buildings. At the narrow raised peak, rows of clerestory windows provide ventilation and light. Expensive to install and maintain, these high windows provide a high level of control over warm and cool air currents and provide excellent natural ventilation. On the Green Wilcox mule barn, these clerestory windows can be opened and closed with a system of pull ropes, but on the later barns at the Henderson Wilcox and Aubrey Bradley farms, the windows are fixed sashes. They can be removed and set aside, but not opened and closed.

The vast size of the Bradley and H. Wilcox barns meant that these high windows seldom needed to be removed for increased ventilation. The monitor roof adds an interesting element to several barns in this part of Randolph County. The design was used earlier by Midge Marshall for his mule barn in Renick and by Guy Cottingham for his barn in the same town, as well as by Henderson Wilcox's brother, Green Wilcox, for his new livestock barn.

Further investigation may uncover the ultimate idea for installing monitor roofs on these barns. Perhaps they were based on these farmers' familiarity with numerous factory buildings in and around Moberly, Missouri's "Magic City" of the late nineteenth and early twentieth centuries, a business center with railroad shops, brick plants, a shoe factory, coal mines, and other industrial buildings. Another possible source for the monitor roofs was the railroad passenger car of the nineteenth and early twentieth century, which typically had a row of clerestory windows on their roofs. Other monitor roofs appear in various parts of Missouri's rural landscape, typically associated large and prosperous farms.

(Above) Recently the Henderson Wilcox barn was sided with sheet metal. The farm is currently owned and farmed by the Wemhoff family. On the neighboring farm to the east, carpenter Walter Bagby had built a large new livestock barn for Wilcox in 1933–34, during the hard times of the Great Depression. Much of the lumber and timbers they used were recycled from demolished railroad bridges. The barn measures circa 75 feet by 160 feet and features the same kind of roof design employed in the mule barn his brother Green Wilcox had built in 1921. (Bob Wilcox, personal communication April 9, 2003)

(Right) The principal difference between Mr. Bradley's barn and earlier transverse-crib barns with clerestory windows is the quality and ingenuity of the barn's construction, and its vast scale. Since Mr. Bradley could provide his own select virgin timber and build the barn larger than his friend Henderson Wilcox, Bradley's barn is often said to be "the best barn in Randolph County." The barn is aligned facing east, perhaps to give more natural light and protection from the weather for morning chores and to facilitate processes of loading the grain bins and hoisting hay in the mow. The wings feature cement block walls to provide added protection from the weather. The Robbs' forty-by-sixty-foot pole barn to the right was built in the 1970s to serve as machine shop and shelter for larger and taller modern farm equipment. (2003)

(Above) Mr. Bradley's older brother, Dudley Lacillus "Lass" Bradley (1889–1955), built this barn on his nearby farm in 1928 to shelter and feed his teams of mules used in the Bradley coal mine. Although it represented a more traditional rendition of the transverse-crib barn type familiar across central and north Missouri, Lass Bradley included certain up-to-date details, such as an increasingly popular gambrel roof and large prefabricated ventilator positioned on top. Gambrel roofs were advertised by the Louden Machinery Company in Iowa: "for a finish to a modern barn, nothing will equal one of the double or gambrel roofs when well built and rightly apportioned."[11] The builder's brother-in-law, Wiley Marshall, played violin for square dances here. (2003)

The barn was large enough to support a variety of activities on a livestock and grain farm of several thousand acres where some three hundred head of horned Hereford cattle were being fed. Inside, there are four interior grain bins flanking the driveway at the front, with a total capacity of fourteen thousand bushels. Next to that, on the north and south sides are halls and stairs to the hayloft. On the south side, there is a workbench (major repairs and blacksmithing jobs were handled at the machine shop at Bradley's coal mine), and across from the shop is a farm office. Beyond and west of those spaces are a series of livestock pens, followed by the feeding areas at the west end of the barn.

(Above) Orb Bradley barn office, (Right) hallway. (2003)

(Above) Barn at Aubrey M. Bradley Jr. farm. (2003)

The Orb Bradley barn's framing system of sawn oak timbers conceptually is identical to the framing in older barns using mortise and tenon construction and pegs. But here, the Boswell brothers used threaded steel bolts instead of carved pegs to fasten principal beams and braces. Galvanized nails were used for smaller joints and other parts of the process. It is interesting to notice that carpenters may readily accept contemporary or new methods (the bolts and nuts) while continuing to adhere to the time-tested floor plan and bracing patterns that have held true for hundreds of years.

Among interesting details are the feeding devices. The barn was built on the site of a productive well that provides water for livestock in bad years as well as good. As in other well-planned barns, grain and hay are fed from directly above. A person could feed the livestock inside the barn without having to change to work clothes.

When Mr. Bradley's son, Aubrey Bradley Jr., built his own barn, he patterned it after his father's. The lumber was produced from his own sawmill. At "Triple J Acres," the last barn the Bradleys built using the same roof design, which seems to have begun with Green Wilcox's 1921 mule barn. Like his father's, its outer walls are built of cement block, and a row of clerestory windows provide illumination and ventilation.

WHAT OTHER QUESTIONS MAY WE ASK ABOUT BARNS?

What other structures may be brought into our rambles down gravel roads bumping across creek fords, our smudged county map or old diary balanced on the dashboard, our cameras, tape recorder, and mud boots at the ready, in search of Missouri's barns?

Through time, some crops have waned to practically nothing (flax, broom corn) and others have utterly disappeared—like hemp. What could we learn about structures associated with the hemp industry before and during the Civil War, at one time vastly important to our young state's economy? Hemp culture and rope-making became a major industry in Little Dixie due to the vast amounts of rope needed in baling cotton.[1] Family stories in Little Dixie tell of the pioneer generation bringing many crops from Kentucky—tobacco plants and seed, cotton, and hemp. Like other crops, hemp was very labor intensive. What became of the warehouses where raw hemp was gathered and stored? Are there any "rope walks" left, perhaps in old towns like Liberty, Lexington, or Glasgow, buildings where hemp fibers were worked into ropes in long narrow rooms and shipped off to New York and Europe?

COTTON

What about the cotton industry, a vital element in Missouri's economy? While today cotton is grown in southeast counties, in the nineteenth century cotton was grown in many others, even in north Missouri. The crop now is picked by machines and taken from the field in special trailers to the gin in town for processing. No special structure is needed on the farm. So the cotton gin and its associated structures become the "barns" we look at in Missouri's significant cotton-growing region in the southeast counties.

Southeast Missouri, 1950s: cotton gin, bales awaiting shipment, near Matthews, New Madrid County. (Photos by Gerald Massie, courtesy Missouri State Archives)

ROUND AND POLYGONAL BARNS

We are fascinated by round and polygonal barns. Rightly so. Our inherited concepts of balance, order, and deep-rooted thinking in rectangles of space are surprised by buildings formed of polygons and circles.

To build a round barn is to seek difference and innovation. Few farmers choose these things, because the business of farming is tied to traditional ways of doing things. Pie-shaped horse stalls and round haylofts defy tradition. But these shapes did attract the minds of a number of leading farmers and builders in the late nineteenth and early twentieth centuries. Some of their photogenic structures remain for us to marvel at and enjoy. There were practical elements in this seemingly odd idea: there is less wall to construct and more usable space in a round hayloft.

Where do these barns come from? As Dr. Becky Snider has shown, here these unusual barns do not stem from pioneer memories of North Carolina or England or Germany. George Washington had a sixteen-sided barn on one of his farms in Fairfax County, Virginia, in 1793, but this unusual example seems to have no bearing on

Missouri examples of the late 1800s. Some are truly round, most are octagonal (eight-sided), and others have even more sides. These barns stem from one of several factors. The shape may reflect a desire for great practicality and economy, or the shape may reflect large and successful farmers' experiments in search of new ideas.[2]

Most of these barns were built in the later years of the nineteenth century and early years of the twentieth century during a time of prosperity and abundance (and before the effects of World War I dampened exuberance for new things). Several hundred round and polygonal barns were built in the Midwest (160 in Iowa alone) and we do not yet know exactly how many were built in Missouri. Snider feels we may have between sixteen and twenty-two surviving examples, based on her research in the files of the Missouri State Historic Preservation Program in Jefferson City.[3]

Within the general circular shape there is variety in how the interior is used and how the roof is supported. Some roofs are self-supporting with no interior vertical posts, but most have central posts to support the roof. Sometimes the silo is in the center of the circle and the roof built around that, offering a solution to supporting a roof on a round building.

(Above) Clark octagonal barn circa 1901 near Rea, Andrew County. (Photo by Jim McCarty)

(Left) Kolkmeyer round barn near Joplin, circa 1907; the lumber was sawn, steamed, and bent on site by the son of Joplin's founder, Jim Cox. (Photo by Jim McCarty)

(Top Two Photos) Davis twelve-sided barn near Leeton, Johnson County, circa 1900; framing. (Photos by Roger Maserang, courtesy Missouri Historic Preservation Program)

Orie Smith round barn, near Kirksville, Adair County, 1917; the barn, 64' in diameter, cost $3-5,000 and employed a lead carpenter and crew for a year. The first floor has spaces for horses, mules, hogs, and cattle and the loft held one hundred tons of hay.[4] The barn is now used for music festivals in the loft with food services offered on the ground floor. (Middle) At time of construction. (Bottom Right) Ground floor interior. (Courtesy Missouri Historic Preservation Program)

Plans for round barns were sold by Louden, Radford, and other companies. Kits could be bought from the Sears and Roebuck catalog and shipped by rail to the nearest town. These barns are an example of "nonregional" vernacular buildings, since designs came from builder's manuals, farm magazines, government pamphlets, agricultural books, and catalogs.

There are no pockets of round barn buildings in Missouri. Instead, they are distributed across the state, found wherever an individual with means and a zest for new ideas decided to have one erected. Round and polygonal barns faded after 1920. Certainly the Great Depression had an adverse effect on farmers' abilities to try new ideas and spend money on novelties. Furthermore, and perhaps just as importantly, new agricultural machinery was not suited to the shapes, and bigger machines from tractors to threshing machines began to have an effect on round and polygonal barn building.

OTHER BARNS AND OTHER STRUCTURES

Among the structures that support the farmer's daily round are the hog house, corncrib, chicken coop, and machine shed. Other outbuildings belong to the work of the house and are clustered there—privy, smokehouse, tank house, washhouse, woodshed. What we see today on most farms represents a great loss of the many small, individual "minor" structures once considered necessary for a farming family.

(Above) The Gilmore octagonal barn, built in 1880 near Ash Grove in Greene County, one of the best-known historic sites in this region is listed on the National Register. It may be the state's only octagonal barn built with stone walls. (Photo by Jim McCarty)

(Left) The Gasconade County Agriculture Association, formed in 1876, created a fairgrounds and constructed several buildings. The Rotunda, designed by Edward Robyn, served as an exhibit hall and has today accrued the stature of a landmark. (2003)

Outbuildings, small and large, suggest the range of other structures. Little Dixie smokehouses, Boone County;

(Above) this one in Audrain County also serves as a "cellar house."

(Top Right) also serves as a washhouse.

(Right) Chicken house, Callaway County, built 1997. (2003)

(Second from the bottom) Granary, Boone County 1974.

(Bottom Photo) Massive modern bins paired with the grain elevator serving both, Marion County. Note the round steel grain bins behind. (Photo by Jim McCarty 2003) As technology changed, corn was shelled before being stored, and corncribs were replaced by bins of various kinds.

With the expansion of technology and the reduction of the old-fashioned family farm, some of these buildings are not needed today. Few families slaughter their own beef, hogs, or poultry. Few smoke ham, bacon, and sausage. Few need a washhouse or a root cellar. The thicket of little buildings necessary and commonplace on Missouri farms is gone. We need to remember the smokehouse and cellar as much as the big red barns, because it is in the details of the farmer's daily round that we learn about the context and range of rural life and economy.

The carriage house was once a prime element in the farmstead of successful families in Missouri. Most towns had a horse barn and show arena, and women's colleges founded before the Civil War still have equestrian programs and historic stables.

(Left) Brick carriage house, stables, and servants' quarters, part of an important historic site in St. Louis, the Campbell House, circa 1857. (1989).

(Bottom Left) At the site of Kenner's Tavern (1819), the first overnight stop west of St. Charles on the Boone's Lick Road, the stables remain. (St. Charles County 2003)

(Top Right Page) Simmons Stables in Mexico (second floor for storing feed) was the largest horse-training barn in the nation when built by Cyrus Clark in 1887. There were one-eighth-mile exercise tracks on east and west sides. (Audrain County 2002) Missouri Preservation (our only statewide nonprofit preservation organization) publishes a list of our "Ten Most Endangered Properties"; the 2003 roster includes the Simmons stable.

(Right Page, Middle Left) Columbia firemen with their horses circa 1906. The firehouse itself is built like a barn and across the street (right rear), a livery stable takes the form of a transverse-crib barn. (Marshall family album)

(Right Page, Middle Right) Stable for horsemanship programs at Stephens College, Columbia. (2002)

(Right Page, Bottom) at William Woods College, in Fulton (Callaway County). (2003)

If we keep our eyes open as we travel, we will spot numerous buildings in rural areas that are "barn-like" structures. But perhaps on the more conservative side, we can find numerous other barn-like structures that seem more to suggest the great practicality of "barns." Churches and public buildings are sometimes described, mockingly perhaps, as "barn-like." The old law school building on the campus of the University of Missouri in Columbia was affectionately known "the law barn." Many structures in the landscape deserve our attention, from country stores to old schoolhouses to camp meeting buildings.

One-room schoolhouses are attractive to rehabilitate and find new uses for. David Burton decided it was important to document country schoolhouses in southwest Missouri. Burton, camera in hand, discovered Greene County schoolhouses that had been converted to barns of various sorts. While some may call this adaptive use, the conversions are not particularly aimed at the conservation of historic buildings but at making use of abandoned buildings. The pragmatist may say that at least these buildings—or their shells—will remain a bit longer. The purist may consider these new uses inappropriate.

(Above) Pavilion on camp meeting grounds of a Protestant church in the Ozarks (Phelps County) is one of the many barn-like structures we see. (2002)

(Left) Leeper School. (Bottom) Mentor School. (1997 photos by David L. Burton, Greene County University Extension, Springfield)

(Above) Old silo, new barn, U.S. 50 near Warrensburg, Johnson County. (Jim McCarty 2003)

(Top Right) On U.S. 54 between Vandalia and Farber, Audrain County 2002.

(Right) North of Hannibal in Marion County. The barn is gone, the abandoned silo remains. (Jim McCarty 2003)

Development of freestanding silos, beginning in the 1880s, altered barn planning in many cases. Most livestock producers had a silo next to their barns where they could turn chopped green cornstalks into "ensilage" to feed animals over the winter. The building of these tall round structures was promoted by farm machinery and construction companies. Silos could be built of beveled wooden staves, but better ones were made from brick, stone, and ceramic tile.

AMISH AND OLD ORDER MENNONITES

Sometimes rural communities retain and use old buildings. The Amish and Mennonite farmers still use their old structures in a number of counties across Missouri. The Amish and Old Order Mennonite rules for daily life and work, as well as worship, are articulated in each district. Each community or district has slightly different rules. However, they share much, including a cohesive system of four-hundred-year-old beliefs and traditions, language that resembles a dialect of German, and a preference to do without most of our modern conveniences. Their development as organized communities goes back to an element of the Protestant Reformation in Europe in the early seventeenth century. Their strict ways and modes of dress and language have sometimes led to misunderstandings, and as they first bought land and began communities in rural Missouri, there was resentment toward them. Yet, like many other Missouri pioneers, they came because of decent, inexpensive farmland and the chance to live according to their own lights.[5]

These groups are famous for their barns and barn raisings. Often they rebuild existing barns on farms they acquire. Other times, they design and build barns. Their reputation is such that these barn-building crews are often hired by outsiders.

(Below and Left) Amish at Jamesport, Daviess County; in this district, barns tend to be painted white. (Photos courtesy Missouri Department of Tourism)

Modern Amish farmsteads often look like those of a hundred years ago. Barns in Audrain County tend to be painted red. Older barns here are usually transverse-crib barns on farms bought from Anglo-Americans, but they are remodeled and expanded. Newer barns tend to take a variation of the English and bank barn types. (Audrain County, photos by John D. Marshall 2003)

Ed McKinney's pole barn, Texas County, a transverse-crib barn plan recalling the hay barn from his childhood. (2003)

MODERN POLE BARNS

For many, the prefabricated barn, made of mass-produced parts assembled on site, is the most familiar barn we know. (We are not speaking here of the pole barn as the term is used for barns made with small skinned trees we saw previously in the Old Mines area.)

For many farmers, a new prefab barn, perhaps in kit form from the local lumber supply outlet, or perhaps erected by a crew of Amish or Mennonite carpenters, is their only practical, affordable option to shelter hay bales, livestock, or a garden tractor. Many of them, while scorned by historians, are old enough to qualify for nomination to the National Register.

Prefabrication is nothing new. Some of the massive timber frame barns that represent the oldest barns in European America are prefabricated structures. Carpenters measured and cut timbers and beams (by sawing or hewing), chiseled mortises and tenons, whittled pegs, then numbered parts with matching Roman numerals chiseled next to assembly points, and then assembled the box like a jigsaw puzzle. The builder of a big hewn-log barn worked up his timber, laid out the parts on the site, and then, with some stout friends, assembled the structure.

In the modern pole barn, major vertical framing members (round or square posts) are set directly in the ground or on concrete pads. But this is not new. "Post-in-ground" or "earth-fast" construction has been part of Missouri's vernacular building tradition since the colonial period—not only among the French but among Anglo-Americans as well who knew post-in-ground buildings in early Virginia, Maryland, and other eastern states. Almost none of these buildings survive.

In the 1970s, Ed McKinney, a history professor and part-time farmer from a pioneer Ozark family, needed a new barn. His pole barn in Yukon, built to Dr. McKinney's specifications, was erected by the Morton Company in 1979 at a cost of $10,500. McKinney selected the cement floor, sheet metal walls and roofing, and other features from the company's literature and a price was agreed upon. The red and white color scheme was the customer's option. McKinney's new barn reflects the plan of the old frame transverse-crib barn on his farm, dating to around 1900, built by Ben Castelman.

Through the nineteenth century, an age of improvement and industrialization, a shift took place from localized, often ethnic and inherited values to more generalized forms and nationalized building patterns. Through those years, prefabrication continued and the factory system grew. Beginning in the 1830s, the availability of cheap wire nails was a technological breakthrough. As nails became increasingly available, the eventual wane of the ancient modes of timber framing with mortise joints was foretold, and the great craft changed from common knowledge to hard-won skills of restoration carpenters and museum experts.[6] We no longer have need for an auger, broadaxe, plane, or foot adze. The two-by-four and the cheap nail are of immense importance, representing a relatively simple technology compared with mortise and tenon timber-frame construction.

In the early twentieth century, manuals and pattern books as well as mail-order catalogs anticipated acceptance of prefab structures shipped from distant factories. In the mid-twentieth century, prefabricated barns took a great leap forward with improved technologies. Experimentation with steel and extruded aluminum, chemical treatment for poles shipped in from the Pacific Northwest, concrete floors, preassembled roof trusses, and the now omnipresent galvanized sheet metal roof and walling grew partly out of wartime industrialization and production methods.

The space between World Wars I and II saw more new technology, with steel Quonset huts and machine sheds with arched or rounded roofs. Various kinds of laminate roof systems were developed. One of the more interesting of these new technologies was the *lamella roof* system, invented and developed in St. Louis in 1925 by Edward Faust. The system is a continuous network of wooden ribs that make a strongly braced arch. Faust hired a German-trained architect, Custel Kiewitt, to build this 50-by-110-foot barn around 1930 in St. Louis County. While the lamella system was economical and stout, it generally disappeared after 1960.[7] Its loss in popularity may have partly been due to its seeming complexity of design, a design perhaps too foreign for the standard barn carpenter and builder of the time.

(Top Two Photos) A lamella roof dairy barn, circa 1930, Chesterfield (St. Louis County 2003). The technology was applied to good effect in sports arenas and convention centers. (Above) The round roof can work on a small barn, too. (Phelps County, photo by Jim McCarty)

(Left) Other twentieth-century roof technologies were more widely accepted by conservative Missouri farmers. The round-arch roof proved accessible to local builders and was comparatively inexpensive. At the Greenley Farm Agricultural Research Center run by the University of Missouri–Columbia in Knox County, the old transverse-crib barn was kept. Next to that they erected a prefab steel building from the Quonset Company. (Knox County 1989)

Prefabrication was central to the federal government's provision of houses, outbuildings and barns for displaced farm workers during the severe drought years following the Stock Market Crash of 1929. Photographers with the Farm Security Administration captured the process of building prefab structures in southeast Missouri. In May 1938 in New Madrid County, Russell Lee photographed a barn raising in the "Southeast Missouri Farms Project." A selection of images from Lee's series documents the process of assembling a prefab barn, beginning with the stacked lumber at the Barn Plant in New Madrid.

Building a prefab transverse-crib barn, 1938, New Madrid County. Panels included sections for a corncrib along one side. (Library of Congress, Russell Lee, Farm Security Administration)

The pole barn with its pine lumber construction will probably need replacement, while a traditionally built barn of seasoned, hewn timbers and mortise and tenon construction will last for hundreds of years if maintained properly. Some observe that pole barn technology has reduced the variety of barns and has simplified barn building so much that buildings lack the imprint of the hand of the old-fashioned carpenter. True. Critics say contemporary prefab pole barns are little more than a sad reminder of a once-beautiful history of skill and virgin timber. But there is more to it. Pole barn technology is efficient, and the necessary skills basic. Many people are able to erect a garden shed or small barn with minimal assistance (if any) from professional crews. An amazing variety of forms, colors, and shapes of pole barns have emerged, reflecting the myriad new purposes and ideas behind their creation.

(Left) Jim McCarty built his blacksmith shop and barn single-handedly in Taos, Cole County. (McCarty photo 2003)

(Bottom Two Photos) On a chilly morning in January at our farm, the animals do not mind if their barn lacks hand-hewn timbers, they just require water, a can of oats, and sanctuary from the weather. (Callaway County 2003).

While this farm in Callaway County may not be typical, it does reflect today's country living and the growing passion to have a place for a few horses (and in this case, a few beef cows, chickens, sheep, fruit trees, and some beehives). The barn was put together in 1989. Founded on the customary transverse-crib plan, the pole barn gets the job done. Since we use net-wrapped big round hay bales that do not require a hay barn, we have none in winter; the cows are fed their morning and afternoon cracked corn in feed bunks (while the sheep scavenge for stray leftovers) and the bales are hauled to steel bale rings on a harpoon attached to the tractor's three-point hydraulic hitch.

Square balers in the 1930s meant the end was foretold for barns with big haylofts and mechanical

devices for loading loose hay. Continuing mechanization brought small round bales and then, in the 1980s and 1990s, big round bales. Lately we see even larger bales produced in rectangles. People continue to use small square bales because they are ideal for a person (especially a part-time livestock producer or equestrian) to feed horses or spread straw for bedding.

New barns, if time, desire, and budget are available, are built using modern materials and devices. From a distance they may look like grand old barns from 1850 or 1900. The Shryock family operates Callaway Farms between Columbia and Kingdom City, and their big red barn was built to current standards to serve their seed, agricultural equipment, and tourism business.

(Right) New Callaway Farms barn, positioned to be visible from I-70, Callaway County. (Photo by Bob McEowen 2002)

FURTHER INNOVATIONS

Missouri is blessed with a number of barns that do not fit the scholar's typologies. Most of these are not vernacular architecture, as usually construed, except in their functions—usually as dairy facilities. A number of outstanding barns were either designed by architects, like Mr. Faust's lamella truss barn, or designs that speak to an owner's desires for "something different." Occasionally, a government agency got involved in barn building, with mixed results.

However, the ancient additive principle of the one-unit structure or single-crib can be detected in virtually any barn—except, perhaps, some of those round barns. Sometimes the expansion of the unit is rather simple, and sometimes exceptionally complex.

(Right) The geometry is almost too dense to quickly decipher in the Lucerne Barn, a famous 1906 dairy barn in Ballwin (St. Louis County) now converted to new uses, including offices, shops, and university classrooms.

(Bottom) Also in St. Louis County, the dairy barn and stable at the Leicester Faust estate in Chesterfield. With stylistic links to Southwestern architecture in New Mexico, his barn illustrates what an owner can do when money is no object. (2003)

(Left and Below) Among Missouri's finest barns are those at Immaculate Conception Abbey (Nodaway County) that supported the abbey and seminary, Benedictine Sisters of Perpetual Adoration (Our Lady of Rickenbach). The Abbey of the Immaculate Conception was founded in 1880 by a Benedictine monk from Switzerland, Father Frowin Conrad. (2003)

The years from the late nineteenth century into the first years of the Great Depression were great years for barn building. State government became active through the University Extension and other agencies in promoting programs they considered to be advances in agricultural technology. Some of the "extension" ideas were superb, others were miserable failures (for example, convincing us to plant multiflora rose along our fields). State university campuses with agricultural science programs, and state agencies such as state hospitals and the prison system, tended to build model barns that projected the latest designs and notions.

(Above) The University of Missouri's booming College of Agriculture built a model dairy barn embracing features of traditional dairy barns with more elaborate layouts and technical features. (University of Missouri Archives)

(Right) Horse and bull barn built in 1937 at Bois d'Arc Cooperative Dairy Farm Historic District near Hughesville, Pettis County; cinder block walls, gambrel roof, and a solid, effective barn design. Government experiments during the Great Depression tried to find ways to provide shelter and a decent living for great numbers of dispossessed people. The Depression caused many farmers to leave the land, often to find their way to the California vegetable farms and orchards in search of work. Most never returned to Missouri. One influential if highly politicized office was the Resettlement Administration (Farm Security Administration), one of Franklin Delano Roosevelt's New Deal agencies, that set about designing and building farmsteads for dispossessed farm families. People moved onto these innovative farms to work in labor collectives, an experiment that drew attention from left and right. New techniques and technologies were tried out, including barn construction materials and methods. One of these projects was Bois d'Arc Cooperative Dairy Farm, part of the Osage Farms properties in Pettis County,[8] listed on the National Register in 1991. (Photo by Roger Maserang, courtesy Missouri Historic Preservation Program)

Farmers continue to experiment. Growers of market vegetables are using a light flexible kind of greenhouse called a "high tunnel" to extend their growing seasons. At the turn of the twenty-first century, most food comes to Missouri grocery stores and restaurants from thousands of miles away, raised on other continents. This realization drives the movement for sustainable farming, a group of young farmers who are using land to raise products ready for farmers' markets or wholesale to specialty grocers. Their places often preserve old buildings while adding new ones suited for specific products. Sustainable agriculture focuses on three principles: The products must be sold in the local community, using home-grown "inputs" like seed and fertilizer from the farm or local community, and the farmer must make enough profit to keep the operation going.[9]

(Right) High tunnel, Callaway County; DeLisa Lewis with her leeks. (2003)

A Note on Mills and Covered Bridges

Old mills—structures that house machinery for grinding wheat, corn, and other crops—are among the most-studied and most-photographed artifacts in our state.

The barn-like mill was where families could have corn and wheat ground for cooking as well as a place where commercial crops could be taken to sell. In some cases in the earlier generations, the mill was also set up to saw lumber on "up and down" or sash saws (distinctive marks of these saws are visible on lumber and timbers in barns). The mill owner typically operated the feed store, and often the post office.

(Top Left and Top Right Photos on Left Page) Dillard Mill, Crawford County. (Photo by Jim McCarty) Bollinger Mill, Bollinger County. (Photo by Jim McCarty) (Bottom Photo on Left Page) Near Gainesville (Ozark County), Hodgson Mill is located near a fresh water spring. The mill stopped in the 1950s, but the company became part of an Illinois firm that continues to sell Hodgson Mill flour, cornmeal and other products made in a modern factory in Gainesville. The mill has been conserved by Hank and Jean Machler, who moved to the Ozarks from St. Louis. They have rehabbed the building and opened a store for selling work by local artists and craftspeople. The mill is a source of pride for many residents who find the rehabilitation and adapted use program well done. The project to save the mill received a Preserve Missouri Award from the Missouri Alliance for Historic Preservation. (Photo by Jeff Joiner)

(Top and Bottom Photos on Right Page) Borgman Mill, 1840, was moved from Marthasville to the Boonesfield outdoor museum near Defiance and awaits restoration. (Bottom) gear axle. (St. Charles County 2003)

(Top and Middle Photos) The Summersville feed mill stands quiet. But inside, most of the machines, belts, shakers, screens, and pulleys are still intact, offering a chance to see equipment of a working mill. The structure, like many mills, is framed like a barn. (Texas County 2003) (Left) Treloar, Warren County, 2003. (Bottom) The Valley Park, built in1895, it survives in conjunction with a hardware store, the last remaining mill in St. Louis County. (2003)

NEIGHBORS *Cowboys of Color*

RURAL
MISSOURI

March 2003

MISSOURI HISTORY *A towering spirit* • GENEALOGY *A detective of his own past*

MISSOURI MADE *A family of basketmakers* • GARDENING *Dream ponds*

HEARTH & HOME *It's Mardi Gras time!*

Like some of our old mills, several covered bridges have been conserved for future generations. The purpose of building a barn-like structure over a bridge was protection of the wooden framework and flooring. With advances in technology in the later nineteenth century and introduction of iron and steel truss bridges to cross big rivers and small creeks, covered bridges became unnecessary. They were expensive to build and difficult to maintain, so covered bridges were only situated on important routes of travel. Apart from special trusses that allowed the bridge to span the distance, and certain technical details, covered bridges were built much like timber frame barns of the early nineteenth century.

The bridges that survive today are in Platte County (near Platte City), Linn County (Locust Creek, near Laclede, a Howe truss bridge from 1868), Union Bridge in Monroe County, Sandy Creek Bridge in Jefferson County, and Bollinger Mill Bridge near Burfordville in Cape Girardeau County.[10]

(Top) Cover March 2003. Locust Creek Covered Bridge in Linn County was located on old Highway 8, the first transcontinental highway across this part of Missouri. (Right) Union Covered Bridge, built in 1871 by Josh Elliott at a cost of $5,000, is 125 feet long. Incorporating an interesting framing and support system, it spans Elk Fork of the Salt River west of Paris and carried traffic between Paris and Fayette. (Monroe County 2000)

Conserving Our Heritage

If you can't put something to a use, it's not going to stay around very long.
A barn sitting out behind an old house isn't going to last very long.
                              —Bill Crawford, Columbia, May 2003

Pockets of old-fashioned log or frame barns probably reflect economic conditions more than a preference for traditional forms handed down through the generations. Because of increased and continuing mechanization and international corporate ownership, the process of growing corn, soybeans, and hogs, from seed to grocery store, is no longer in the hands of farmers. Larger and larger operations replace small family farms that once were the backbone of the nation's economy.

(Left) Mrs. Anna Bernice Vernon painted scenes from her pioneer family's story, "Migrating to Missouri." (1974)

(Right) Calves, Randolph County 2003.

(Below) Red barn, Adair County 1990.

The historic farmstead reflected marvels of nineteenth- and twentieth-century engineering. Changes brought prosperity to some people. Today we wonder at the wholesale removal of the original agricultural landscape by farming that is highly mechanized and industrialized. Yet perhaps no less drastic was the swaths of prime farmland taken by strip-mining coal operations and today's pallet and pressed board industry that clears off great reaches of Ozark timber. Add the well-meaning federal agencies that demolished hundreds of historic farmsteads (including some of the most important historic buildings in Missouri) for the sake of flood control and providing dams and lakes for public recreation. Such are the kinds of topics we find ourselves pondering when we think about the rural landscape that made Missouri attractive to the pioneers.

(Top Left) "Doc Baker's Barn," Boone County, by Leland Schaperkotter. (Courtesy Boone County Historical Society)

(Middle Left) Barn suffocated by urban expansion, Boone County 2003.

(Bottom Left) Barn, working, Moniteau County 2003.

(Above) Barns (granaries), future unknown, Pike County 2003.

(Right) Barn, Callaway County 1994, destroyed.

State documentation of the historic buildings and archaeological sites offers examples of how to study old buildings. The Cultural Resources Office in the Missouri Department of Transportation records and studies options for sites scheduled to be rubbed out by highway improvements. It is almost always a losing proposition. "Heavy traffic, increased real estate values, ubiquitous business establishments, and improved transportation facilities along this corridor have contributed to the demise of the Richterkessing farms and their agricultural setting."[1] Those words summarize the future of a great many historic sites and landscapes across Missouri, many of them languishing, abandoned, falling in, animals nesting in the roof, littered with beer cans and trash, death sentences sealed.

That leaves us with documentation, often a gloomy job. Together with good historical research, the key is often taking time to photograph, measure, and in other ways document buildings and sites. Perhaps our efforts may help future generations understand. We hope so. But time slips by. I drove past the Richterkessing farms for fifty years, glancing over and smiling at the houses' beautiful brickwork, enjoying the barn's Meramec Caverns roof. Then one day, history was gone and concrete had covered it over. Field research is all that remains.[2]

Other old farmsteads receive new life as public places. In Boone County, the nineteenth-century farm of the Lenoir and Nifong families has been given new life as a town park operated by Columbia Parks and Recreation. The 1877 house "Maplewood" was built by Slater Lenoir, whose parents came from North Carolina in the 1830s. Listed on the National Register, this is an important site where the Boone County Historical Society gives tours and the community hosts festivals. The brick house was refurbished during the nation's Bicentennial in 1976. Most farmsteads of this vintage have been lost or altered beyond recognition.

(Above) "Maplewood" is an example of the house type favored by early Little Dixie families from Virginia, North Carolina, Kentucky, and other upland Southern states. (Boone County 2003)

(Left) Quarters and summer kitchen have somehow survived despite difficult social issues the building may suggest; originally unpainted, in 2003 it is barn red with white trim.

Carriage house at Maplewood, then and now. The building contained quarters for a hired hand. (Right) Loading loose hay (1910). (Courtesy of Boone County Historical Society)

(Above) Frame stock barn from the 1870s in the form of a four-crib-type barn. (2003)

(Left and next page Right) The "big barn," a transverse-crib, originally had vertical battens and trim painted white; and today as Maplewood Barn Theater. (Courtesy of Boone County Historical Society)

(Right) The Boone County Historical Society built headquarters in 1988 near the farm buildings and designed their structure to suggest the county's heritage of barns and rural living. (2003)

Photographers and photo collectors sometimes give us the best context for understanding change and time.

(Above) Mrs. C. H. Kroeger in her yard below the Supreme Court building circa 1910. From historic photograph collection amassed by Dr. Joseph S. Summers and published by his daughter, Dottie Dallmeyer in *Jefferson City, Missouri*. (Courtesy Dottie S. Dallmeyer)

(Left) Albert Conrad Lutz's blacksmith shop, Flint Hill, 1899. Left to right: Confederate Army veteran named Boehmer; Romanis Hermann (child in rear), Elmer Carl Lutz, Conrad Albert Lutz, Albert Conrad Lutz with his hammer; other names not known. Ron Lutz, radio announcer, musician, and for some forty-four years host of the weekly "Rooster Creek Show" (KFAL-AM, Fulton), remembers his grandfather's blacksmith shop in Flint Hill (St. Charles County). As a child, Ron would visit his grandparents and sleep on a featherbed upstairs above the forge. In the early morning he could smell his grandmother's freshly ground Old Judge coffee. To Ron, the whole building was a thrilling place of magic and personal meaning. "I could smell history." The massive timbers in the forge "were huge," hewn out with a broadaxe, "and blackened from time." Ron has the broadaxe. The building was bulldozed a few years ago to make way for some new buildings. (Courtesy Ron Lutz)

(Above) Barn with a new purpose, Interstate 70, Warren County 2003.

(Right) Adaptive use. Dairy barn converted to apartments by Fern and Everett Payne, near Seymour (Webster County). (Photo by Jim McCarty)

Lewis Baumgartner of rural Millersburg (Callaway County) calls himself "The World's Worst Farmer" in his series of after-dinner talks and magazine columns. A good storyteller and leader in the community, Baumgartner with keen humor tells of his trials and tribulations farming in "Cocklebur County."

THERE'S NO LIGHTS ON IN THE BARN

Not so many years ago,
If you were to take a ride,
Across America's farmland
And thru the countryside;

If by chance your ride should happen,
As the day was nearly done,
Most every farmstead on the road,
Would have the barn lights on.

The farmer and a kid or two,
Or maybe even more.
Each one busy with a task,
Doin' up the evenin' chores.

Milk the cow, feed the chickens
And gather up the eggs.
Throw some hay down from the loft
And water the sow and pigs.

Sometimes my mind will wander back,
And recall those days, now gone,
Of peaceful winter evenings,
With *The Lights On In the Barn.*

The smell of all the cattle,
Mixed with the grain and hay.
To me it was a pleasing smell,
Though it may not sound that way.

And while filling up the water tank,
I'd watch the cats at play.
A nearly perfect ending,
To another busy day.

Then gazing toward the house,
I could see the kitchen light,
Momma's fixin' supper,
To feed us all tonight.

And the warm glow from that window,
Made this country boy work hard,
To get in to that apple pie
And that chicken, fried in lard.

But the trend today is larger,
And fewer family farms.
Not so many places left now,
With *The Lights On In the Barn.*

They tell us that it's progress,
That nothin' stays the same.
We must look toward the future,
And not the past from where we came.

And I know, that is true,
But tell me, what's the harm?
If I feel a twinge of sadness,
'Cause *There's No Lights On In the Barn.*

Everything is gettin' big,
And no one seems alarmed,
That the chickens and the hogs now,
Are mostly raised on Factory Farms.

We've taken out the fences,
And . . . the barn . . . it's been torn down.
It takes a lot of room,
To turn 16 rows around.

My favorite memories take me back,
To the way we used to farm.
And to peaceful winter evenings,
With *The Lights On In the Barn.*

Mr. Baumgartner's barn advertises, "Baumgartner—World's Worst Farmer," but he is far from it. (2002)

Many barns are burned to the ground as practice sites by rural fire departments. Many other barns are bulldozed by agencies in the belief that forests and conservation areas must be cleansed of any trace of the people who once lived there. Many barns have been rubbed out by the weather. We cannot understand barns or even view photos of barns without wondering whether we could do better in looking after our inheritance. Why does a successful nation encourage its people to destroy their own history?

(Above and Below) Before and after. David Dunn handsomely restored his barn near Bourbon (Crawford County). (Photos by Jim McCarty)

(Above) Barn along Interstate 55, Perry County. (Photo by Jim McCarty 2003)

(Left) The Treisch farm is thought to have been settled by Ernst August Treisch (1811-1873), part of a family of 1850s German immigrants from Saxony. The log buildings, including the log double-crib barn and dogtrot house, may have been built earlier and purchased by the Treisches. Faust Park professionals judge the site to be the last intact 1850s German farmstead in St. Charles County.[3]

(Above) In Independence, the Oscar Schowengerdt farm was sold in the 1950s as another subdivision came to the area. The barn was converted to commercial uses and today is the last remaining barn amongst urban sprawl. (Jackson County 2003)

(Rigth) Silo Ridge Golf and Country Club, Bolivar, Polk County. (Photo by Brian Genovese 2003)

(Bottom Right) Dr. Ed McKinney, from a pioneer Ozarks family, is a model for thoughtful, informed Missourians who care about history; he is an excellent keeper of his family farm (including the 1900 Ben Castelman transverse-crib barn), genealogy, and local history. (Yukon, Texas County 1991)

One innovative program is "Barn Again!" Projects are selected in annual contests sponsored by *Successful Farming* and the National Trust for Historic Preservation to recognize families who preserve and continue to use historic farm buildings. Promoting adaptive use of old buildings is an important trend. Many older barns will not continue to be used as they were intended, so farmers are finding ways to keep the buildings while adapting them to contemporary purposes. The Barn Again! Program also assists owners of barns, publishes barn preservation information, sponsors workshops, and has helped several states with preservation programs.[4]

Sometimes a tremendous building is saved for the future through sheer luck. The 1820 Van Horn Tavern in western Boone County, several miles west of Columbia, a structure of great historic importance, has for many years been used as a barn. Built in 1820, this seems to be the last surviving log tavern and stage stop on the Boone's Lick Road, originally a trail running from St. Charles to the Boone family's 1804 saltworks near Franklin on the banks of the Missouri River in Howard County. At Franklin, trails to Santa Fe and the Oregon country began. Travelers coming by foot, horse, and wagon typically camped at taverns, resting and feeding their animals. If finances allowed, they could rent a bed for a night's sleep. Taverns were also the focus of community meetings, religious gatherings, and everything from voting to marriage ceremonies.

(Left and Above) Van Horn Tavern, an 1820 log dogtrot house on the Boone's Lick Road in western Boone County, on a cool day in April 2003 when the annual mating ritual of buzzards is taking place on the roof. Drawing closer, we become eager to see the log walls behind the inconspicuous barn siding.[5] Like many taverns, this was the residence for the owner's family. A number of historic figures stayed here, such as writer Washington Irving and Senator Thomas Hart Benton. Van Horn owned the tavern until he died in 1865. The tavern remained in business until the 1880s, in the time when railroads were beginning to carry most of the travelers and nearby towns sprouted hotels near depots.

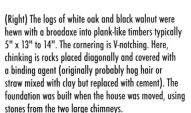

(Right) The logs of white oak and black walnut were hewn with a broadaxe into plank-like timbers typically 5" x 13" to 14". The cornering is V-notching. Here, chinking is rocks placed diagonally and covered with a binding agent (originally probably hog hair or straw mixed with clay but replaced with cement). The foundation was built when the house was moved, using stones from the two large chimneys.

(Above) When the dogtrot house was put back together in 1914, the house/tavern/stage stop was set on a stone foundation and shed additions were added. The structure was placed on the edge of a hill so it could function like a bank barn, with a stable for milk cows on the downhill slope. The north side now lacked its large chimney, and that gap was enlarged to allow hay to be loaded into what was once a parlor.

(Right) The Missouri Folklore Society's logo is a sketch of a barn drawn by Cathy Barton of Boonville, circa 1975. The Society seeks to study and conserve the state's many facets of traditional culture, music, and folklife.

Among other programs that help bring attention to historic farms is the University of Missouri–Columbia's Century Farms project. To be on the list, a farm needs to have been in the same family for one hundred years, include at least forty acres of the original land, and make a financial contribution to the farm income. Honorees receive a special sign to mark their farm.[6]

Images of barns continue to have meaning throughout daily life. In 2002, when graphic artist Shannon Allmon prepared a new set for the "Pepper and Friends" daily television show on KOMU-TV in Columbia, she painted a red barn and hung the painting prominently.

Television show host Paul Pepper with Shannon Allmon's painting. (2003)

THE FARM VS. THE TOWN

If farmers knew the ups and downs
Of people living in the towns,
Without a job, their money spent,
No cash to pay for food or rent,
And scarcely funds enough to go
To see the latest movie show,
Twould change the views they've often had,
And farming would not seem so bad.[7]

—T. F. Fulkerson

(Top) Boone County fair 1974.

(Above) Farm, St. Charles County 2003.

On our long lists of barns and barn-like structures we appreciate, we could also place a parade of barns that just look good. They may feature painted messages or scenes. They may exhibit eye-catching construction. They merely may be strong and straight and worthy.

(Left) "Hopedale Farm." (Photo by Ralph Walker, Courtesy Missouri State Archives)

(Below) "The Arrival at the Croy Farm in 1867." (Courtesy Missouri State Archives)

(Upper Right and Above) Owned by Dr. Donald Kuenzi, this Century Farm barn is located east of Helena in Andrew County. The restoration of the barn was completed in 2001 and the barn has been featured in *Successful Farming Magazine* as well as the *Barn Again! Program.* (Scott Rule 2003)

(Right) Osage County. (Photo by Jim McCarty)

If we continue demolishing old buildings willy-nilly, whole chapters of our national experience will be lost. Cultural conservation encourages us to treat history as living heritage instead of trying to freeze-dry the past behind museum glass or perfectly restored mansions. Doing this means we try to capture all records of a building, from intangible memories to sources such as courthouse records and wills.

Get involved and document the old farmsteads in your community. Free advice and assistance are available from agencies such as the Missouri Historic Preservation Program (P.O. Box 176, Department of Natural Resources, Jefferson City, MO 65102), cultural resources staff of the Missouri Department of Transportation (P.O. Box 270, Jefferson City, MO 65102), and the statewide citizens' group, Missouri Alliance for Historic Preservation (P.O. Box 1715, Columbia, MO 65205 www.preservemo.org).

ENDNOTES

CHAPTER 1

1. *Compact Edition of the Oxford English Dictionary* (1971), p. 765; for additional discussion of the word, see for example H. L. Mencken, *The American Language* (1919, 1977), p. 136 and various encyclopedias. In thinking about barns in their place in the history of agriculture, one or two books about agriculture itself may be helpful; for example, E. and F. Schapsmeier, *Encyclopedia of American Agricultural History* (1975) and J. Schlebecker, *Whereby We Thrive: A History of American Farming, 1607–1972* (1975).

2. I studied English, Welsh, Irish and particularly Lowland Scots farm buildings as part of my research as a professor at the University of Missouri–Columbia. While a number of visits were made in the 1980 and 1990s, most of my studies took places in 1993 and 1994 when I recorded historic buildings in the central Scottish Lowlands between Glasgow and Edinburgh as a Visiting Research Fellow in the European Ethnological Research Centre in the National Museums of Scotland (Edinburgh). In addition to development of a traveling exhibition for communities in the region, some of the research was published; "British Isles—Subregion—Upper Avon River Valley (Central Scotland)," and "Estate Worker's Housing (Scotland)," in Paul Oliver (ed.), *Encyclopedia of Vernacular Architecture of the World*.

3. *Oxford English Dictionary, ibid.* Sometimes the usages are still with us, but their actual history forgotten—like the expression "barn-burner," heard in television sports commentary to describe a hotly contested game. "Barn burner" comes from newspaper writing in the 1840s, when the radical wing of the Democratic Party wanted to destroy corporations and banks that were guilty of unethical business practices. These "barn burners" (among them the feisty red-haired Martin Van Buren) took their name from the old story of the Dutch farmer who, in a valiant but misplaced effort to rid his barn of rats, which consumed his crops, burned his barn to the ground. No more rats, and no more barn. And we have "barn-stormers." This great expression began in medieval England as a description for strolling thespians, jesters, and musicians who wandered the city streets and, on a moment's notice, were apt to produce impromptu performances in barns.

4. Walter Williams, *The State of Missouri* (1904), p. 58.

5. C. and E. Chapman, *Indians and Archaeology of Missouri* (1983), p. 49.

6. Chapman, op. cit., throughout; this is perhaps the best brief work on Missouri's Native American heritage; also see R. Wood and R. McMillan, *Prehistoric Man and His Environments* (1976), W. Klippel, "Graham Cave Revisited (1971), and especially M. O'Brien and Wood, *The Prehistory of Missouri* (1998). For broader views see P. Nabokov and R. Easton, *Native American Architecture* (1989) and W. Morgan, *Prehistoric Architecture in the Eastern United States* (1980).

7. Chapman, pp. 53, 67.

8. Chapman, pp. 83–84; also Nabakov and Easton, "Native Americans" p. 21.

9. Chapman, p. 101; the first recorded contact with the French was in 1720 on the Missouri River in central Missouri (p. 99); also p. 108 for description of Osage houses and the food storage pits located inside. See Chapman passim, and Chapman, "Osage Indians in Missouri and Oklahoma," in Wyckoff and Hoffman, *Pathways to Plains Prehistory*, 19–28. Also see Rollings, *The Osage* and Baird, *The Osage People*.

10. See Meyer, *The Heritage of Missouri*, p. 128 ff.; Gilbert, *The Trail of Tears across Missouri*, Bealer, *Only the Names Remain: The Cherokees and the Trail of Tears*, and Ehle, *Trail of Tears: The Rise and Fall of the Cherokee Nation*. Trail of Tears State Historic Site is located near Cape Girardeau. Tahlequah, Oklahoma, is the location of tribal headquarters for the Cherokee Nation, and the Trail of Tears National Historic Trail (National Park Service) conserves and interprets the saga of the Cherokee, Chickasaw, Choctaw, Creek, Seminole, and other tribes removed to Oklahoma Indian Territory. The author appreciates help from Herschel Price, superintendent at Trail of Tears State Park (2003). Also see Porter, "American Indians in the Eastern United States," in Noble, *To Build in a New Land*.

Reader's Note: Interest in old barns flourished in the 1960s and 1970s due to the appearance of a number and variety of publications, such as Eric Sloan's wonderfully illustrated books, most famously his 1967 *An Age of Barns*, and to Arthur and Witney's handsome 1972 art book (*The Barn*). Detailed, carefully researched field studies, such as those by Fred Kniffen and Henry Glassie, helped make a place for "old barns" in the academic world. Glassie's intensive ethnographic and theoretical studies remain models have been widely influential. Alongside these books came many good and helpful studies during the years of the United States Bicentennial in 1976. Studies appeared that focused on small areas or specific barn types, such as the work of people like John Fitchen, Amos Long, Alfred Shoemaker, Tom Hubka, Keith Sculle, and Wayne Price, Peter Ennals in Canada, and Nigel Harvey and Walter Horn in England. Two books that helped bring popular attention to the study and preservation of barns are Sloan's *An Age of Barns* (1967) and Arthur and Witney's *The Barn* (1972), and a new compilation of Library of Congress archival photos by Vlach (*Barns*, 2003) gives an overview of American barns.

By most reckonings the most stimulating examinations of barns are Henry Glassie's articles in the 1960s and 1970s such as "Barn Building in Otsego County, New York," a loving examination of a single county. Since the golden age of rediscovering our rural past, there have come dozens of books and articles on barns in Europe, the United States, and Canada, ranging from the tourist pocket guide to art books of fine photographs to the scholars' research-based studies. The bulk of publications on American barns pertain to New England, the upland South, and states such as Ohio, Pennsylvania, and Indiana. It is in those areas where a number of active researchers and writers have been based through the past forty years. A number of articles and books contain material on barns, while addressing larger issues of cultural geography, architectural history, and folklife.

A number of useful surveys and publications do exist for Missouri, such as Dr. Becky Snider's work on round and octagonal barns, this author's survey of the Little Dixie region, and the several excellent surveys of historic sites such as that conducted by Professor Tom Carneal at Northwest Missouri State University in the 1980s. Though a landmark from the 1960s, Caldwell's *Missouri Historic Sites Catalogue* is fat with houses but thin in barns, listing only several structures such as the Pony Express Stables in St. Joseph (1858) and several mills. Apart from examples that include van Ravenswaay's *Arts and Architecture of German Settlements in Missouri*, this author's *Folk Architecture in Little Dixie* and 1986 articles recording the Pelster family's Germanic housebarn in Franklin County, and Becky Snider's article on round and octagonal barns in *Missouri Folklore Society Journal*, rather little has been published specifically to analyze barns of the Show-Me State.

CHAPTER 2

1. For discussion of vernacular building, see Brunskill, *Traditional Buildings of Britain* (p. 24), "Vernacular Building" (p. 167); Roberts, "Folk Architecture"; Glassie, *Pattern in the Material Folk Culture of the Eastern United States* and *Folk Housing in Middle Virginia*; Rapoport, *House Form and Culture* (1969); and this author's *Folk Architecture in Little Dixie* (pp. 17–29) and *Vernacular Architecture in Rural and Small Town Missouri*.

2. For the *single-cell* house type, see Marshall, *Folk Architecture in Little Dixie* and "The British Isles Single-Cell House in the American Cultural Landscape," *Folk Life: Journal of Ethnological Studies*. The basic British-American house is a one or one-and-one-half-story one-room single-cell (single-pen) house with chimney centered in the gable end and opposed front and rear doors. Many log cabins built in pioneer times were well built and represented temporary economics, not temporary architecture. Almost all log cabins were covered with horizontal weatherboarding to protect the log walls, provide added insulation, and present the look of a frame building. Institutions that reconstruct and preserve log cabins usually do not include the original weatherboarding and thus the log walls deteriorate faster.

3. A good overview is J. Joiner, "By Way of a Barn" (1992).

4. Barn plans have been commercially produced for more than two hundred years; among the more notable are Allen's *Rural Architecture* (1852) and *Rural Architecture* (1860), Halstead, *Barn Plans and Outbuildings* (1881), and W. Radford, *Radford's Practical Barn Plans* (1909); recently, consumers may plan their barns using such publications as Progressive Farmer Magazine's *Barns: Farm Shops and Outbuildings* (1997).

Barn hayloft in Randolph County, formerly on Highway 63, south of Jacksonville. (Pat B. Clark)

CHAPTER 3

1. For building in Little Dixie, a cultural region of Missouri, see Marshall, *Folk Architecture of Little Dixie*, "Little Dixie," in Wilson and Ferris, *Encyclopedia of Southern Culture* and "Midwest—British, Subregion—Little Dixie (Missouri), in Oliver, *Encyclopedia of Vernacular Architecture of the World*, as well as J. Denny, "A Transition of Style in Missouri's Antebellum Domestic Southern Architecture," *P.A.S.T.: Proceedings of the Pioneer America Society*, "Early Southern Domestic Architecture in Missouri, 1810–1840," *P.A.S.T.* (1985) and "The Georgian Cottage in Missouri," *P.A.S.T.* (1989).

2. Roberts showed that it could take as many as seventy-five different tools to make a log house or barn completely from scratch. Roberts, "The Tools Used in Building Log Houses in Indiana" and *Log Buildings of Southern Indiana*.

3. Scandinavian settlers in the Delaware Valley in the seventeenth century brought their own distinctive methods of horizontal log construction, but these modes did not become a part of the Missouri log-building story. We have seen log houses (no barns) built by Scandinavian immigrants in north Missouri coal-mining camps of the later nineteenth and early twentieth century, but such log-working traditions appear to be quite rare and perhaps found nowhere else in the state. Perhaps future research will fill in this gap in our knowledge. Scholars disagree about whether German-speaking immigrants or Scandinavian immigrants exerted the most influence on "the American log cabin" (we tend to line up with the Germans on this question).

4. Numerous books and articles explain tools, timber frame and log construction; e.g. Mercer, *Ancient Carpenter's Tools*; Hindle, *America's Wooden Age*; Kniffen and Glassie, "Building in Wood"; Glassie, *Pattern in the Material Folk Culture of the Eastern United States*; Roberts (op. cit.); Kauffman, *American Axes*; and perhaps most enjoyable are Sloane's books such as *A Museum of Early American Tools*. Also see Marshall, *Folk Architecture in Little Dixie*. The broadaxe and broad hatchet (hewing hatchet) both have chisel-like blades sharp on only one side. The broadaxe is heavier, weighing six to nine pounds, and has a longer handle. Often, but not always, the handle of the broadaxe is offset or bent away from the head so the hewer may work along the side of a log without endangering hands, legs, and feet. The hewing hatchet is lighter, handier, and usually honed sharper than the broadaxe, and used by the crew foreman or master carpenter to do finishing and cleaning up of the hewing after the basic hewn log was derived. Sometimes the term "shingling hatchet" is confused with broad hatchet, since the tool can be used, like the froe, for splitting out shingles. Hewing hatchets were not made for driving nails. In many cases, only the heavier broadaxe was used for log walls, and in the hands of a master axe man, the finished surface of the log wall was perfect. Most broadaxes found today at auctions and antique malls are of late nineteenth or twentieth century vintage and made in the "western" or "American pattern." Factory-made versions of cast steel were sold through catalogs such as Sears and Roebuck. Many were purchased at the hardware store. Many more were made by a local blacksmith of hand-forged iron. Broadaxes and hatchets can still be purchased from specialty tool catalogs. All are descendents of broadaxes used in colonial times in Virginia, and the lineage goes back to ancient times in Europe.

5. The venerable global practice of using pegs to secure joints gave rise to the expression "a square peg in a round hole." In fact, one *wants* a square peg in a round hole; it does not seem to fit at the beginning because the peg is carved just a little larger than the hole but carved squarish and when the wood is green. The peg is driven through the hole in the lined up tenon and mortise with a wooden mallet. The greenness of the trunnel makes it flexible enough to be forced into the hole. When the peg dries, it dries to an extremely tight fit inside the augured hole through the joint.

6. See for example Tishler, "The Site Arrangement of Rural Farmsteads" and Stipe, *New Directions in Rural Preservation*.

CHAPTER 4

1. L. Basler, *A Tour of Old Ste. Genevieve* (1975); good pages on the French appear in McCue and Peters, *A Guide to the Architecture of St. Louis* (1989).

2. Peterson 1941, p. 222. The barn type is called an "Acadian barn"(*grange Acadien*) in the St. John Valley of Maine; as across the river in Canada, the typical Acadian barn in northern Maine (grange Acadien) of the early period is a three-bay side-opening gable-roof threshing barn much like the so-called "English" barn. See Brassieur, *The Maine Acadian Cultural Survey*.

3. Personal communication, Ms. Billie Mills, Perryville, 25 April 2003. John Baptist de la Salle (1651–1719) was a French Roman Catholic cleric in Rheims who founded the Christian Brothers teaching order in 1684 to train teachers to establish schools for children of the poor. De la Salle was a distinguished educator. Victor Javeaux and his cohorts undoubtedly were trained in Rheims. The 1930s photo of the Javeaux barn appears in J. Vlach, *Barns*, p. 239 (in addition to other Missouri barns photographed by the Historic American Buildings Survey and other projects housed at the Library of Congress).

4. See Thurman, *Building a House in Eighteenth Century Ste. Genevieve* and the writings of Peterson.

5. Good places to start in understanding the French are Dorrance, *The Survival of French in the Old District of Ste. Genevieve*; Peterson, "Early Ste. Genevieve and Its Architecture"; parts of van Ravensway's 1941 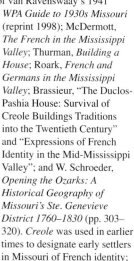*WPA Guide to 1930s Missouri* (reprint 1998); McDermott, *The French in the Mississippi Valley*; Thurman, *Building a House*; Roark, *French and Germans in the Mississippi Valley*; Brassieur, "The Duclos-Pashia House: Survival of Creole Buildings Traditions into the Twentieth Century" and "Expressions of French Identity in the Mid-Mississippi Valley"; and W. Schroeder, *Opening the Ozarks: A Historical Geography of Missouri's Ste. Genevieve District 1760–1830* (pp. 303–320). *Creole* was used in earlier times to designate early settlers in Missouri of French identity; later the term took on racial connotations (Brassieur, "Expressions," p. 2 ff.).

6. Peterson's 1941 article includes terms still somewhat familiar in Ste. Genevieve, such as *terrain* (village lot), *emplacement* (palisaded enclosure around farm yards), stable (*etable*; *ecurie*), shed (*hangard*), hen house (*poulailler*), corncrib (*cabane a mahis*), and oven (*four*); Ste. Genevieve people, higher in social and economic status than the miners, did not like the *cabanes* (cabins) the Old Mines people built in the manner of Anglo-American log cabins.

7. Much has been done to study Cajun houses (linked to Missouri Creole houses) but less has been done with barns; the "Cajun barn" as delineated by Comeaux with a single log crib set back from the front of the surrounding additions ("Cajuns in Louisiana," pp. 183–185) does not seem to appear in Missouri.

8. Ray Brassieur, personal communication, 10 April 2003.

9. *The WPA Guide to 1930s Missouri* , p. 531; also see W. Schroeder, *Opening the Ozarks* (2002), p. 348–349.

10. For this area, see Skaggs, "Rural Life in Madison County," Williams, *State of Missouri*, pp. 438–439. It is too early to say that large hay bonnets mean French farmers, since they are distributed through areas of early Anglo-American as well as German settlement.

Brian barn. (photo by Jim McCarty)

Chapter 5

1. The classic delineation of the English/double-crib barn was developed by Professor Glassie in seminal publications such as *Pioneer America*, "The Double-Crib Barn" (Jan. 1969, July 1969, Jan. 1970, July 1970) and *Pattern in the Material Folk Culture of the Eastern United States.*

2. Fuller documentation of this important farmstead, see T. Prawl, "The W. L. Cornett House" (1986) and Marshall, "The Sisters Leave Their Mark." It is hoped the fabulous collection of family belongings as well as the buildings will be conserved by the College of Agriculture for the benefit of future generations.

3. The best-known Anglo-American communities in Missouri are the Protestant British planters in the central part of the state, the Irish in St. Louis, and the numerous Scotch-Irish in rural settlements in the Ozark geographic region.

4. For Little Dixie history, material culture, and vernacular building, see Marshall, "Mr. Westfall's Baskets: Traditional Craftsmanship in North Central Missouri" (1974) in J. Brunvand, *Readings in American Folklore* (1979); "Meat Preservation on the Farm in Missouri's Little Dixie" (1981), "Little Dixie" in Wilson and Ferris, *Encyclopedia of Southern Culture* (1989); "Marmaduke's Hornpipe," *Missouri Folklore Society Journal*, (1991–92). James Denny's studies of Federal-era houses are essential; see "A Transition of Style in Missouri's Antebellum Domestic Southern Architecture," *P.A.S.T.: Proceedings of the Pioneer America Society* (1984); "Early Southern Domestic Architecture in Missouri, 1810–1840: The 'Georgianization' of the Trans-Mississippi West," *P.A.S.T.: Proceedings of the Pioneer America Society* (1985); "The Georgian Cottage in Missouri: An Obscure but Persistent Alternative to the I-House in the Upper South," *P.A.S.T.: Proceedings of the Pioneer America Society* (1989); and see D. Sheals, "British-American Stonework in Mid-Missouri: A Study in Vernacular Architecture" (1993) and L. Sparks, "The Burton-Wight House and the Bruns House: Vernacular Architecture and Ethnicity on the Missouri Frontier" (1994). Other treatments of aspects of the region include D. Hurt, *Agriculture and Slavery in Missouri's Little Dixie* (1992).

5. Important Ozarks research is available by scholars such as Carl Sauer and Vance Randolph, and more recently Robert Flanders, Russel Gerlach, Lynn Morrow, and Milton Rafferty. The Scotch-Irish, who arguably provided the largest portion of the early white population of frontier Missouri, are understudied and confused in much of the literature; see Rafferty, *Missouri Geography*, pp. 65 ff; also *The Ozarks: Land and Life* and *Immigrants to the Ozarks*; Sauer, *Geography of the Ozark Highland of Missouri*. Part of the confusion is due to misinformation about their actual origins, with many today lumping the Ulster Scots together with other people from Ireland — a common practice dating from the earliest immigration to America. The reputation of these people as feisty, independent frontiersmen is supported in history, and the Scotch-Irish themselves like to feed the mythology (Bob Holt, Ava, personal communication, Dana Everts-Boehm, April 1992).

6. van Ravenswaay, *Arts and Architecture* p. 274.

7. "Bergt Farm Complex," National Register of Historic Places Inventory Form (1979), Missouri Historic Preservation Program. The National Register of Historic Places (part of the National Park Service in the Department of Interior) is the nation's official list of structures, sites, and districts that have been documented and declared worthy of preservation. Sites are nominated through offices in each state for listing on the Register, and countless properties have yet to be documented and nominated. In Missouri, the National Register process and related processes are handled by the State Historic Preservation Program in Jefferson City.

8. Old farms in Warren County can be researched through such publications as the 1885 *History of St. Charles, Montgomery, and Warren Counties, Missouri.* Many counties reprinted these classic histories (which can be selective and impressionistic), available in such places as the Reference Room of the State Historical Society of worthy of preservation. Sites are nominated through offices in each state for listing on the Register, and countless properties have yet to be documented and nominated. In Missouri, the National Register process and related processes are handled by the State Historic Preservation Program in Jefferson City.

Chapter 6

1. Exact prototypes in the Old World are hard to find; "the bank barn resulted from a meshing of the multilevel banked barn notion from Central Europe and northwestern England with the double-crib barn idea from Central Europe." (Glassie, "The Double-Crib Barn in South Central Pennsylvania," Part 4 (1970), pp. 23–34.)

2. My thanks to Ms. Billie Mills of Perryville for helping me understand this barn (2003).

3. See p. 17 in A. Hesse and M. South, *Gasconade County Tours*, van Ravenswaay, *Arts and Architecture*, p.285–287 and Wells, *Barns in the U.S.A.*

4. Slit vents are sometimes called "arrow slits" and "rifle slits," thinking that farmers stood inside and shot arrows and guns at folk, a notion founded in fact but flavored by legend. The slits often are positioned out of reach, and the opening is a bit narrow.

5. Stone is found in every Missouri county. "Rock" technically is unworked stone and fieldstone; "stone" is cut and worked into building material. The great stone houses and barns in St. Charles, Osage, and Gasconade Counties are the result of the settler's luck in finding plentiful, workable limestones and dolomites. Many settlers and builders knew how to work with stone. In places where good stone is available, often we find no farm buildings made of the material. Why? Did they not come from a stone working tradition, or did they prefer the predominant American modes of wood or brick? Where settlers came from a strong tradition of brick — southeastern England, the Virginia Tidewater, parts of Europe — entire barns were erected of brick. Typically, brick was made on site, but later in the nineteenth century railroads brought in brick fired in plants in cities.

6. Photographed by the Historic American Buildings Survey as part of their recording of historic sites in Missouri.

7. Debbie Oakson Sheals, "British-American Stonework in Mid-Missouri: A Study in Vernacular Architecture."

8. The Hosmen information is found in the National Register documentation in the Missouri Cultural Resources Inventory, Missouri Historic Preservation Program, Missouri Department of Natural Resources, Jefferson City.

9. Louis T. Sohn Barn Survey Report, Cultural Resources, Missouri Department of Transportation, Jefferson City. Names of barn crewmembers recalled were Ganzer, Scherrer, Roth, and Krause. Like the National Register survey forms, MoDOT cultural resources survey forms are a valuable source for the historian and preservation planner.

10. The best brief look at this barn type is chapter three in Arthur and Witney's *The Barn*; also see Dornbusch and Heyl, *Pennsylvania German Barns*; Long, *The Pennsylvania German Family Farm*; Ensmiger, *The Pennsylvania Barn*; writings of Glassie such as "The Pennsylvania Barn in the South" (1965–1966) and *Pattern in the Material Culture of the Eastern United States*, and writings of Noble such as *The Old Barn Book*. These and other scholars have disagreed over the final definition of *Pennsylvania barn,* but we agree on basic ingredients of forebay, ramp, and two-level plan with livestock below. The added detail of an *unsupported* forebay is a debated element.

11. Carneal, survey of historic sites in northwest Missouri (ms.), Northwest Missouri State University, Maryville, 1980–1981.

12. Many feel Germanic culture in Missouri flourished in only a few counties along the Mississippi and Missouri Rivers from below St. Louis up and west to around Jefferson City. Carneal's discovery of the Ozenberger bank barn demonstrates that generalizations need continual revision when new research is produced.

13. Among publications are Bergey, "The Pelster Housebarn: A German-American Landmark in Missouri"; Marshall, "The Pelster Housebarn: Survival and Rejuvenation of Germanic Architecture" (*The German-American Experience in Missouri*); Marshall, "The Pelster Housebarn: Endurance of Germanic Architecture on the Midwestern Frontier"; van Ravenswaay's *Arts and Architecture of German Settlements*; and Chapell, "Germans and Swiss" (Upton, *America's Architectural Roots*).

CHAPTER 7

1. The barn type was proposed by Kniffen in "Folk Housing: Key to Diffusion" (1935) as the dominant barn type across the upland South and most areas to which the region sent emigrants; for Little Dixie, see Marshall 1981, etc.

2. See Sparks, "The Burton-Wight House and the Bruns House: Vernacular Architecture and Ethnicity on the Missouri Frontier"; Waller, *History of Randolph County*; Marshall, *Little Dixie* and *Old Families of Randolph County, Missouri*.

3. Prawl and Sone, "The Ralph Richterkessing Farm: An Expression of German-American Culture in Rural Missouri," *Missouri Folklore Society Journal*. The outstanding documentation is featured on the Historic American Buildings Survey pages of the Library of Congress "American Memory."

4. See M. Broggie's engaging book, *Walt Disney's Happy Place*.

5. *Missouri and Tobacco* (1960), p. 5; for more scholarly writing, see D. Hurt, *Agriculture and Slavery in Missouri's Little Dixie* (1992), passim.

6. In 1904, Williams in *The State of Missouri* could list tobacco in every Missouri county except Douglas. Statistics can be surprising, considering the tobacco agriculture in different counties in 2003; counties reporting more than 50 acres were Boone 71, Barry 64, Bollinger 65, Callaway 139, Carroll 248, Cedar 56, Chariton 750, Dallas 54, Franklin 60, Holt 55, Howard 69, Howell 102, Monroe 51, Saline 104, Schuyler 164, Stoddard 57, Stone 60, Taney 64, Texas 58, and Wright 60. Jasper County and St. Louis County reported 2 acres each, and Mississippi and New Madrid, 1 each.

7. *Missouri and Tobacco*, p. 1 ff. Many a child has experimented with smoking behind the barn or in the hollow—and usually with disenchantment—with such handy plants as native grapevine or a hank of corn silk.

8. I documented the Jacobs house in 1974 and a photo of it appears in *Folk Architecture of Little Dixie* p. 84. For excellent discussion of tobacco and related matters see Hurt, *Agriculture and Slavery in Missouri's Little Dixie*.

9. On his second voyage to the New World in l493, Christopher Columbus brought asses (donkeys) to the New World, and they spread throughout Spanish colonial America. Descendents of Columbus's donkeys were bred to large draft horses from Europe and the eastern United States to produce the Missouri mule. A mule is the sterile, hybrid offspring of a male donkey and a female horse, bred as a work animal. See Bradley, *The Missouri Mule: His Origins and Times*; Bradley and Dailey, *Recollections of Missouri Mules*; and Marshall, "The Complicated Legacy of the Missouri Mule."

10. *Louden Barn Plans*, p. 24.

CHAPTER 8

1. A good overview of hemp is chapter 5, Hurt, *Agriculture and Slavery in Missouri's Little Dixie*.

2. Snider, "The Round Barn Form: Functionality, Spiritualism, or Aesthetics?"; for some round barn builders such as the Shakers in New England the shape was spiritual, but this factor does not seem to apply to Missouri examples; also see W. McGilevry, "The Ozarks Octagon Stone Barn"; Sculle and Price, "Barns of Nonorthogonal Plan"; and chapter five in Arthur and Witney, *The Barn*.

3. Snider, pp. 13, 18.

4. L. England, "It's in the Round," and "Orie J. Smith Black and White Stock Farm Historic District" (Missouri Historic Preservation Program files, Jefferson City). There are circa 160 round and polygonal barns on the National Register.

5. An excellent introduction is Hartman, "Old Order Amish and Old Order Mennonites in Missouri" in Marshall and Goodrich, *The German-American Experience in Missouri*.

6. Among reviews of developments in nail manufacture is Stewart, "The Nail Trade in Missouri: Archaeological Evidence at the Hickman

House" and Nelson, "Nail Chronology as an Aid to Dating Old Buildings."

7. "The Faust Estate," courtesy Jesse Francis, O'Fallon.

8. "Bois d'Arc Cooperative Dairy Farm Historic District" (Missouri Historic Preservation Program files, Jefferson City). These government programs were considered "wildly impractical and patently un-American, an inspired approach to the farm problem that helped thousands of families survive the Great Depression, or something in between." Considered by many people to be socialist programs, in 1943 Congress abolished them.

9. For more on this topic, *Small Farm Today* (3903 W. Ridge Trail Road, Clark, MO 54243).

10. Local lore surrounds the old covered bridges, with stories of courting couples meeting in secret. A darkened covered bridge offered highwaymen an excellent spot to rob travelers. These buildings are museum pieces; they carry nostalgia and romantic images of the past.

CHAPTER 9

1. We are grateful that agencies have people like Dr. Prawl and her colleagues in their employ. See Prawl and Sone, "The Ralph Richterkessing Farm: An Expression of German-American Culture in Rural Missouri," p. 48 ff. The Richterkessing project combined staff at MoDOT with the Missouri State Historic Preservation Office and Federal Highway Administration and work was done to meet requirements of Section 106 of the National Historic Preservation Act and Section 4(f) of Department of Transportation regulations.

2. Architectural survey methods involve general traverses of an area, with note-taking and photography, followed by investigation and recording of specific sites selected for importance or relevance to the history of the community and questions at hand. Documentation from surveys has value for future researchers and archives, and libraries, as reference material describing conditions in a time and place. With recording the physical scene and the landscape itself, field methods include oral interviews and discussions with knowledgeable citizens. One may also contact the National Trust for Historic Preservation (1785 Massachusetts Avenue NW, Washington, DC 20036, www.nationaltrust.org). See McKee, *Recording Historic Buildings*. Also see Stipe, *New Directions in Rural Preservation*.

3. Courtesy Wayne Gronefeld and Jesse Francis 2003. The site is under the care of the Howell Foundation, committed to preserving historical assets, assisting community youth in achieving goals, and providing a foundation for future leaders.

4. Address: Barn Again!, National Trust for Historic Preservation, 910 16th Street Denver, CO 80202 (www.barnagain.org); publications include pamphlets such as *Barn Again!: A Guide to Rehabilitation of Older Farm Buildings*, *Barn Foundations*, and *New Spaces for Old Places*. See Humstone, "The Best Way to Save a Barn Is to Put It Back to Work," *Successful Farming*.

5. See D. Sapp, *The 1820 Route of the Boone's Lick Trail Across Boone County, Missouri* (2000) and C. Watson, *A Remnant of the Booneslick Trail* (2001), pp. 1–16. Daniel Boone's sons Nathan and Daniel Morgan, and their partners, developed the salt works in Howard County in 1805, where they boiled salty spring water in large iron cauldrons to produce salt. As the water evaporated, salt settled in the bottom of the kettles. Salt was a valuable commodity and necessary staple of the pioneer diet. It took 250–300 gallons of brine water to produce a bushel of salt. The Boone-Morrison Saltworks operated until 1833, but was shut down during the Indian troubles during the War of 1812. A trail from St. Charles to the saltworks became known as the "Boone's Lick Trail." See Darrough, *Boone County Album*, Crighton, *A History of Columbia and Boone County*, and Gordon, "The Ishmael Van Horn Tavern."

6. Application forms and more information are available from local Extension Offices, the University's Century Farm office in Columbia (573-882-7216), and from Extension Publications (2800 Maguire Boulevard., Columbia, MO 65211).

7. T. F. Fulkerson, Moberly, from his "Christmas Greetings" poems mailed to family and friends in the winter of 1933–34. (Author collection)

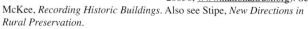
Barn near Lebanon, MO. (photo by Jim McCarty)

Livingston County, south of Chillicothe. (photo by Scott Rule)

- 157 -

West of Cameron, DeKalb County. (Pat B. Clark)

BIBLIOGRAPHY

Arthur, Eric and Dudley Witney. *The Barn: A Vanishing Landmark in North America*. Greenwich, Conn.: New York Graphic Society, 1972.

Auchley, W. J., David Barker, and Peggy Oliver Rodgers. *A Pictorial History of Montgomery County*. Virginia Beach, Va.: The Donning Company Publishers, 1993.

Baird, David W. *The Osage People*. Phoenix, Ariz.: Indian Tribal Series, 1972.

Barley, Maurice W. *The English Farmhouse and Cottage*. London: Routledge and Kegan Paul, 1961.

Basler, Lucille. *A Tour of Old Ste. Genevieve*. Ste. Genevieve: Wehmeyer Publishing Company, 1975.

Bealer, Alex W. *Only the Names Remain: The Cherokees and the Trail of Tears*. Boston: Little, Brown, 1972.

_____. *Old Ways of Working Wood*. New York: Crown Publishers reprint, 1980.

Bergey, Barry. "The Pelster Housebarn: A German-American Landmark in [Franklin County] Missouri." *Gone West!* 1 (summer 1983), pp. 5–11.

Bradley, Melvin. *The Missouri Mule: His Origins and Times*. 2 vols., Columbia, University of Missouri Extension Division, 1993.

_____ and Duane Dailey. *Recollections of Missouri Mules*. 13 vols., Columbia, University of Missouri Extension Division, 1991.

Brassieur, C. Ray. "The Duclos-Pashia House: Survival of Creole Buildings Traditions into the Twentieth Century." *Material Culture* 22:2 (1990), pp. 15–25.

_____. "Expressions of French Identity in the Mid-Mississippi Valley." Dissertation, University of Missouri–Columbia, 1999.

Broggie, Michael. *Walt Disney's Happy Place*. Virginia Beach, Va.: The Donning Company Publishers, 2001.

Brunskill, Ronald W. *Vernacular Architecture of the Lake Counties*. London: Faber and Faber, 1978.

_____. *Traditional Buildings of Britain*. London: Victor Gollancz, Ltd., 1982.

Burnett, Robyn and Ken Lubbering. *German Settlement in Missouri: New Land, Old Ways*. Columbia: University of Missouri Press, 1996.

Caldwell, Dorothy J. *Missouri Historic Sites Catalogue*. Columbia: State Historical Society of Missouri, 1963.

Chapman, Carl H. *The Archaeology of Missouri I*. Columbia: University of Missouri Press, 1975.

_____. *The Archaeology of Missouri II*. Columbia: University of Missouri Press, 1980.

_____. "Osage Indians in Missouri and Oklahoma." In D. Wyckoff and J. Hoffman, *Pathways to Plains Prehistory* (1982), 19–28.

_____ and Eleanor F. *Indians and Archaeology of Missouri*. 1964, Revised ed., Columbia: University of Missouri Press, 1983.

Comeaux, Malcolm L. "Cajuns in Louisiana." In A. Noble (ed.), *To Build in a New Land: Ethnic Landscapes in North America* (Baltimore: Johns Hopkins University Press, 1992), pp. 177–192.

Condit, Carl W. *American Building: Materials and Techniques from the First Colonial Settlements to the Present*. Chicago: University of Chicago Press, 1968.

Crichton, John C. *A History of Columbia and Boone County*. Columbia: Computer Color-Graphics, 1987.

Dakin, Ralph and Barbara. *Historic Sites of Mid-Missouri Painted by Ralph Dakin*. Marceline, Mo.: Walsworth Publishing Company, 2001.

Darrough, James. *Boone County Album*. Columbia: Boone County Sesquicentennial Committee, 1971.

Denny, James M. "A Transition of Style in Missouri's Antebellum Domestic Southern Architecture." *P.A.S.T.: Proceedings of the Pioneer America Society* 7 (1984), pp. 1–11.

_____. "Early Southern Domestic Architecture in Missouri, 1810–1840: The 'Georgianization' of the Trans-Mississippi West." *P.A.S.T.: Proceedings of the Pioneer America Society* 8 (1985), pp. 11–22.

_____. "The Georgian Cottage in Missouri: An Obscure but Persistent Alternative to the I-House in the Upper South." *P.A.S.T.: Proceedings of the Pioneer America Society* 12 (1989), pp. 63–70.

_____. "The Irish Wilderness: The Curious History of an Ozarks Place." *Ozarks Watch* 5:3 (winter 1989), 80–82.

Dornbusch, Charles H. and John K. Heyl. *Pennsylvania German Barns*. Allentown: Pennsylvania German Folklore Society, 21, 1958.

Dorrance, Ward A. "The Survival of French in the Old District of Ste. Genevieve." Columbia: *University of Missouri Studies Quarterly* 10:2 (1935).

Dregni, Michael. *The Old Barn: A Treasury of Family Farm Memories*. Stillwater, Minn.: Voyageur Press, 2002.

Edwards Brothers. *Illustrated Historical Atlas of Boone County, Missouri*. 1875, reprint, Columbia: Geneaological Society of Central Missouri, 1991.

Edwards, Jay D. "French." In D. Upton, *America's Architectural Roots* (Washington: Preservation Press, 1986), pp. 62–67.

Ehle, John. *Trail of Tears: The Rise and Fall of the Cherokee Nation*. New York: Anchor Books, 1989.

Ekberg, Carl J. *Colonial Ste. Genevieve: An Adventure on the Mississippi Frontier*. Gerald, Mo.: Patrice Press, 1985.

England, Lori. "It's in the Round." [Kirksville round barn] Truman State University, New Media Index web site October 14, 1999, http://index.truman.edu/issues/19992000/1014/features/features14.asp

Ensminger, Robert F. "A Search for the Origins of the Pennsylvania Barn." *Pennsylvania Folklife* 30:2 (winter 1980/81), pp. 50–71.

_____. *The Pennsylvania Barn: Its Origin, Evolution and Distribution in North America*. Baltimore, Md.: Johns Hopkins University Press, 1992.

"The Faust Estate: A History." Manuscript, Chesterfield, Mo.: Faust Historical Village, n.d.

Flader, Susan, ed. *Exploring Missouri's Legacy: State Parks and Historic Sites*. Columbia: University of Missouri Press, 1992.

Flanders, Robert. "Caledonia: Ozark Legacy of the High Scotch-Irish." *Gateway Heritage* 6:4 (spring 1986), pp. 34–52.

Gerlach, Russel L. *Immigrants in the Ozarks: A Study in Ethnic Geography*. Columbia: University of Missouri Press, 1976.

_____. "The Ozark Scotch-Irish." In M. Roark, *Cultural Geography of Missouri* (Cape Girardeau: Southeast Missouri State University, 1983), pp. 11–29.

_____. *Missouri Geography*. Boulder, Colo.: Westview Press, 1983.

_____. *Settlement Patterns in Missouri*. Columbia: University of Missouri Press, 1986.

Gilbert, Joan. *The Trail of Tears across Missouri*. Columbia: University of Missouri Press, 1996.

Glassie, Henry. *Pattern in the Material Culture of the Eastern United States*. Philadelphia: University of Pennsylvania Press, 1968, 1977.

_____. "The Old Barns of Appalachia." *Mountain Life and Work* 40:2 (summer 1965), pp. 21–30.

_____. "The Pennsylvania Barn in the South." *Pennsylvania Folklife* 15:2 (winter 1965–1966), 8–19; 15:2 (summer 1966), pp.12–25.

_____. "The Double-Crib Barn in South Central Pennsylvania." *Pioneer America* Part 1 (1:1, January 1969), 9–16; Part 2 (1:2, July 1969), 40-45; Part 3 (2:1, January 1970), 47–52; Part 4 (2:2, July 1970), pp. 23–34.

_____. "The Variation of Concepts within Tradition: Barn Building in Otsego County, New York." In H. G. Walker and W. G. Haag (eds.), *Man and Cultural Heritage: Essays in Honor of Fred B. Kniffen* (Baton Rouge: Louisiana State University School of Geoscience, 1974), pp. 177–235.

_____. "Barns Across Southern England: A Note on TransAtlantic Comparison and Architectural Meanings." *Pioneer America* 7:1 (1975), pp. 9–19.

_____. "Eighteenth-Century Cultural Process in Delaware Valley Folk Building." *Winterthur Portfolio* (1972), reprinted in Dell Upton and John Michael Vlach (eds.), *Common Places: Readings in American Vernacular*

Livingston County (courtesy of MoDOT)

Architecture (Athens: University of Georgia Press, 1986), pp. 394–425.

_____. *Vernacular Architecture*. Bloomington: Indiana University Press, 2000.

Goodman, William L. *The History of Woodworking Tools*. New York: D. McKay, 1966.

Gordon, Tricia. "The Ishmael Van Horn Tavern." *Columbia Senior Times* (August 2001).

Gregg, Kate L. "The Boonslick Road in St. Charles County." *Missouri Historical Review* 27:4 (July 1933), pp. 307–324.

Grove, Carol Edwards. "The Foursquare House Type in American Vernacular Architecture." Masters thesis, University of Missouri, Columbia, 1992.

Halstead, Byron David. *Barn Plans and Outbuildings*. New York: Orange Judd, 1881, 1891, 1906, 1909.

Hart, John Fraser. *The Look of the Land*. Englewood Cliffs, N.J.: Prentice-Hall, 1975.

Harvey, Nigel. *A History of Farm Buildings in England and Wales*. Newton Abbot, England: David and Charles, 1970.

_____. *Old Farm Buildings*. Aylesbury, Bucks: Shire Publications, 1975, 1987.

Hawkes, Pamela W. "Economical Painting: The Tools and Techniques Used in Exterior Painting in the 19th Century." In Jandel (ed.), *The Technology of Historic American Buildings* (1983), pp. 189–220.

Hesse, Anna Kemper. *Centenarians of Brick, Wood and Stone: Hermann, Missouri*. Hermann, Mo.: Brush and Palette Club, 1969.

_____, ed. "Hermann, 1895–1920: A Golden Era of German-American Culture in Missouri." Manuscript, Hermann, 1991.

_____. *Little Germany on the Missouri: The Photographs of Edward J. Kemper, 1895–1920*. Columbia: University of Missouri Press, 1998.

_____ and Mary South. *Gasconade County Tours*. Hermann: [no publisher given], 1975.

Hill, George G. "Practical Suggestions for Farm Buildings." *Farmer's Bulletin No. 126* (Washington. D.C., U.S. Department of Agriculture, 1903).

Hindle, Brooke. *Technology in Early America*. Chapel Hill: University of North Carolina Press, 1966.

_____, ed. *America's Wooden Age: Aspects of Its Early Technology*. Tarrytown, N.Y.: Sleepy Hollow Restorations, 1975.

_____, ed. *Material Culture of the Wooden Age*. Tarrytown, N.Y.: Sleepy Hollow Press, 1981.

History of St. Charles, Montgomery, and Warren Counties, Missouri. St. Louis: National Historical Company, 1885.

History of Warren County, Missouri. 1885, reprint, Warrenton: Warren County Historical Society, 1993.

Hoard, Robert J. and Toni M. Prawl. "The Origins and Evolution of Rock Fences in Missouri." *Material Culture* 30:1 (1998), pp. 1–22.

Hodgkinson, Ralph. *Tools of the Woodworker: Axes, Adzes, and Hatchets*. Nashville, Tenn.: American Association for State and Local History, Technical Leaflet 28, 1965.

Holden, Bob. "In Missouri, Preservation Makes Economic Sense." *National Trust Forum* 17:1 (fall 2002).

Hopkins, Alfred. *Modern Farm Buildings*. New York: McBride, Nast, 1913.

Houck, Louis. *A History of Missouri*. 3 vols. Chicago: R. R. Donnelly & Sons, 1908.

Hubka, Thomas. "Barns." In Diane Maddex (ed.), *Built in the U.S.A.: American Buildings from Airports to Zoos* (Washington: Preservation Press, 1985), pp. 24–27.

Humstone, Mary. "Round Barn Winners." *Progressive Farmer* April 1999.

_____. "The Best Way to Save a Barn Is to Put It Back to Work." *Successful Farming* May 2001.

Hurt, Douglas R. *Agriculture and Slavery in Missouri's Little Dixie*. Columbia: University of Missouri Press, 1992.

Innocent, Charles F. *The Development of English Building Construction*. Cambridge: Cambridge University Press, 1916.

Jandl, H. Ward, ed. *The Technology of Historic American Buildings*. Washington: Association for Preservation Technology, 1983.

Joiner, Jeff. "By Way of a Barn." *Rural Missouri* (September 1992), p. 19.

Jordan, Terry G. and Matti Kaups. *The American Backwoods Frontier: An Ethnic and Ecological Interpretation*. Baltimore, Md.: Johns Hopkins University Press, 1989.

Kauffman, Henry J. *American Axes: A Survey of Their Development and Their Makers*. Brattleboro, Vt.: Stephen Greene, 1972.

Klippel, Walter E. "Graham Cave Revisited: A Re-evaluation of Its Cultural Position During the Archaic Period." *Memoir of the Missouri Archaeological Society* 9 (1971).

Kniffen, Fred. "Louisiana House Types." Annals of the Association of American Geographers 26 (1936), pp. 179–193.

_____. "The American Covered Bridge." *Geographical Review* 41 (1951), pp. 114–123.

_____. "Folk Housing: Key to Diffusion." 1965, reprint in D. Upton and J. Vlach (eds.), *Common Places* (op. cit.), pp. 3–26.

_____ and Henry Glassie. "Building in Wood in the Eastern United States: A Time-Place Perspective." 1966, reprint in D. Upton and J. Vlach (eds.), *Common Places* (op. cit.), pp. 159–181.

Land Atlas and Plat Book Callaway County Missouri 1995. Rockford, Ill.: Rockford Map Publishers, 1995.

Landmarks Association of St. Louis. *From Kerry Patch to Little Paderhorn: A Visit in the Irish-German Communities of Nineteenth Century St. Louis*. St. Louis: 1966.

Long, Amos, Jr. *The Pennsylvania German Family Farm*. Breiningsville, Pa.: Publications of the Pennsylvania German Society, No. 8 (1972).

Louden Machinery Company. *Louden Barn Plans*. Fairfield, Iowa, 1915.

McAlester, Virginia and Lee. *A Field Guide to American Houses*. New York: Knopf, 1984.

McCarty, Jim. "Burley: Tobacco is a Family Crop." *Leisure Time*, September 2, 1984, pp. 4–9.

_____, ed. *The Day the Lights Came On*. Jefferson City, Association of Missouri Electric Cooperatives, 2000.

McCue, George. *Bingham's Missouri*. St. Louis: St. Louis Mercantile Library Association, 1975.

_____ and Frank Peters. *A Guide to the Architecture of St. Louis*. Columbia: University of Missouri Press, 1989.

McDermott, John F. *A Glossary of Mississippi Valley French, 1673–1850*. St. Louis: Washington University Studies No. 12 (1941).

_____, ed. *The French in the Mississippi Valley*. Urbana: University of Illinois Press, 1966.

McGilevry, William. "The Ozarks Octagon Stone Barn." *Ozarks Mountaineer* 34 (May–June 1986), 38–39.

McKee, Harley J. *Recording Historic Buildings*. Washington: U.S. National Park Service, 1970.

Maddex, Diane, ed. *Built in the U.S.A.: American Buildings from Airports to Zoos*. Washington: National Trust for Historic Preservation, 1985.

Marling, Karal Ann. *Tom Benton and His Drawings*. Columbia: University of Missouri Press, 1985.

Marshall, Howard Wight. "Mr. Westfall's Baskets: Traditional Craftsmanship in Northcentral Missouri." *Mid-South Folklore* 2:2 (1974), pp. 43–60. Reprinted in J. Brunvand (ed.), *Readings in American Folklore* (New York: Norton, 1979).

_____. "The Concept of Folk Region in Missouri: The Case of Little Dixie." Dissertation, Indiana University, Bloomington, 1976.

_____. *American Folk Architecture: A Selected Bibliography*. Washington: Library of Congress, American Folklife Center, 1981.

_____. *Folk Architecture in Little Dixie: A Regional Culture in Missouri*. Columbia: University of Missouri Press, 1981.

_____. "The Pelster Housebarn: Survival and Rejuvenation of Germanic

Chaney barn (photo courtesy of Missouri State Archives)

Architecture." Chapter in H. Marshall and J. Goodrich (eds.), *The German-American Experience in Missouri* (Columbia, Publications of the University of Missouri Cultural Heritage Center, 1986), pp. 61–83.

_____. "The Pelster Housebarn: Endurance of Germanic Architecture on the Midwestern Frontier." *Material Culture* 18:2 (1986), pp. 65–104.

_____. "The Sisters Leave Their Mark: Folk Architecture and Family History." In Robert Walls, et al. (eds.), *The Old Traditional Way of Life: Essays in Honor of Warren E. Roberts* (Bloomington, Ind.: Trickster Press, 1989), pp. 208–227.

_____. "The Complicated Legacy of the Missouri Mule." *Agricultural Libraries Information Notes*, Vol. 15, No. 3 (March 1989), pp. 1–12.

_____. "The British Isles Single-Cell House in the American Cultural Landscape." *Folk Life: Journal of Ethnological Studies* (U.K.), Vol. 28 (1989–1990), 31–40 and Vol. 29 (1990–1991), pp. 97–98.

_____. "Little Dixie." In Charles Wilson and William Ferris (eds.), *Encyclopedia of Southern Culture* (Chapel Hill: University of North Carolina Press, 1989), pp. 572–573.

_____. "Aspects of German-American Vernacular Architecture in Hermann: Patterns of Retention and Acculturation." (manuscript) Hermann: Missouri Humanities Council Symposium, 1992.

_____. *Vernacular Architecture in Rural and Small Town Missouri.* Columbia: University of Missouri Extension Division, 1994.

_____. "Vernacular Housing and American Culture." In Ruth Brent and Benyamin Schwarz (eds.), *American Popular Housing* (New York: Greenwood, 1995), pp. 1–40.

_____. "Vernacular Architecture." In Jan H. Brunvand (ed.), *American Folklore: An Encyclopedia* (New York: Garland, 1995), pp. 41–44.

_____. "Cultural Landscape." In Jan H. Brunvand (ed.), *American Folklore: An Encyclopedia* (New York: Garland, 1995), p. 182.

_____. *Paradise Valley, Nevada: The People and Buildings of an American Place.* Tucson: University of Arizona Press, 1995.

_____. "Vernacular Architecture." In Jan H. Brunvand (ed.), *American Folklore: An Encyclopedia* (New York: Garland, 1996), pp. ___.

_____. "Midwest—British, Subregion—Little Dixie (Missouri)." In Paul Oliver (ed.), *Encyclopedia of Vernacular Architecture of the World* (Cambridge: Cambridge University Press, 1997), pp. ___.

_____. "British Isles—Subregion—Upper Avon River Valley (Central Scotland)." Chapter in Oliver (ed.), *Encyclopedia of Vernacular Architecture of the World* (ibid.).

_____, ed. *Old Families of Randolph County, Missouri: A People's History.* Moberly: Randolph County Historical Society, 1976.

_____ and James A. Goodrich, ed. *The German-American Experience in Missouri.* Columbia: University of Missouri Cultural Heritage Center and University Extension Division, 1986.

_____ and Walter Schroeder. "Introduction." *Missouri: The WPA Guide to the "Show-Me" State.* 1941; reprint, St. Louis: Missouri Historical Society, 1998, pp. ix–xxiv. Also in 1986 reprint, *The WPA Guide to 1930s Missouri* (Lawrence: University Press of Kansas). Massey, Ellen Gray, ed. "Mules—The Foundation of the World." *Bittersweet Country* (Garden City, N.J.: Anchor Press, l978), pp. 74–82.

Mencken, H. L. *The American Language.* 1919; reprint New York: Alfred A. Knopf, 1977.

Mercer, Henry Chapman. *Ancient Carpenter's Tools.* Doylestown, Pa.: Bucks County Historical Society, 1960.

Meyer, Duane. *The Heritage of Missouri: A History.* St. Louis: State Publishing Co., 1973.

Missouri State Historic Preservation Office. Cultural Resources Inventory. Jefferson City, Mo.: Missouri Department of Natural Resources. http://www.cr.nps.gov/nr/

Morgan, William N. *Prehistoric Architecture in the Eastern United States.*
Boston, Mass.: M.I.T. Press, 1980.

Nabakov, Peter and Robert Easton. *Native American Architecture.* New York: Oxford University Press, 1989.

Nagel, Paul C. *Missouri, a Bicentennial History.* New York: W. W. Norton, 1977.

Nelson, Lee. "Nail Chronology as an Aid to Dating Old Buildings." Nashville: American Association for State and Local History, Technical Leaflet 48 (1968).

Noble, Allen G. "Barns and Square Silos in Northeast Ohio." *Pioneer America* 4:2 (July 1974), pp. 12–21.

_____. "The Evolution of American Farm Silos." *Journal of Cultural Geography* 1:1 (fall–winter 1980), pp. 138–148.

_____. *Wood, Brick, and Stone: The North American Settlement Landscape Volume 2: Barns and Farm Structures.* Amherst: University of Massachusetts Press, 1984.

_____, ed. *To Build in a New Land: Ethnic Landscapes in North America.* Baltimore, Md.: Johns Hopkins University Press, 1992.

_____ and Richard K. Cleek. *The Old Barn Book: A Field Guide to North American Barns & Other Farm Structures.* New Brunswick, N.J.: Rutgers University Press, 1995.

_____ and Hubert G. H. Wilhelm. *Barns of the Midwest.* Athens: Ohio University Press, 1995.

O'Brien, Michael J., Robert E. Warren, and Dennis E. Lewarch. *The Cannon Reservoir Human Ecology Project.* New York: Academic Press, 1982.

O'Brien, Michael J. and W. Raymond Wood. *The Prehistory of Missouri.* Columbia: University of Missouri Press, 1998.

O'Brien, Mike. "Picture Perfect: Renovation of Ozark County's Hodgson Mill Renews One of Missouri's Mot-photographed Sites." *Springfield News-Leader*, February 23, 2003. http://news.ozarksnow.com/email_thanks.html

Parker, Paul E. *A Portrait of Missouri 1935–1943: Photographs from the Farm Security Administration.* Columbia: University of Missouri Press, 2002.

Parrish, William E., Charles T. Jones, Jr., and Lawrence O. Christensen. *Missouri: Heart of the Nation.* St. Louis: Forum Press, 1980.

Peters, J. E. C. *The Development of Farm Buildings in Western Lowland Staffordshire up to 1900.* Manchester, England: Manchester University Press, 1969.

_____. *Discovering Traditional Farm Buildings.* Princes Risborough, Bucks: Shire Publications, 1981.

Peterson, Charles E. "Early Ste. Genevieve and Its Architecture." *Missouri Historical Review* 35:2 (January 1941), pp. 207–232.

_____. "The Technology of Early American Building. Association for Preservation Technology, *Newsletter*, 1 (April 1969), pp. 3–17.

_____. *Colonial St. Louis: Building a Creole Capital.* Tucson, Ariz.: Patrice Press, 1993.

_____, ed. *Building Early America: Contributions toward the History of a Great Industry.* Radnor, Pa.: Chilton Book Co., 1976.

Peterson, Fred W. *Homes in the Heartland: Balloon Frame Farmhouses of the Upper Midwest, 1850–1920.* Lawrence: University Press of Kansas, 1992.

Prawl, Toni M. "The W. L. Cornett House, Linn County, Missouri: Cultural Expression and Family History through Architecture and Furniture, 1884–1986." Thesis, University of Missouri, Columbia, 1986.

_____ and Stacy Sone. "The Ralph Richterkessing Farm: An Expression of German-American Culture in Rural Missouri." *Missouri Folklore Society Journal* 22 (2000), pp. 27–52.

Radford, William A., ed. *Radford's Practical Barn Plans.* Chicago: New York: Radford Architectural Co., 1909.

Rafferty, Milton D. *Atlas of the Ozarks.* Springfield, Mo.: Aux-Arc Research Association, 1980.

Above photo courtesy of Cultural Resources, Missouri Department of Transportation, Jefferson City.

_____. *Missouri Geography*.

_____. *The Ozarks: Land and Life*. Norman: University of Oklahoma Press, 1980.

Roark, Michael, ed. *French and Germans in the Mississippi Valley: Landscape and Cultural Traditions*. Cape Girardeau: Center for Regional History and Cultural Heritage, Southeast Missouri State University, 1988.

_____. "Storm Cellars: Imprint of Fear on the Landscape." *Material Culture* 24:2 (1992), pp. 46–47.

Roberts, Warren E. "The Tools Used in Building Log Houses in Indiana." 1977. Reprint in D. Upton and J. Vlach (eds.), *Common Places* (op. cit.), pp. 182–202.

_____. *Log Buildings of Southern Indiana*. Bloomington, Ind.: Trickster Press, 1984.

Roe, Keith E. *Corncribs: In History, Folklife and Architecture*. Iowa City: University of Iowa Press, 1988.

Rollings, Willard H. *The Osage: An Ethnohistorical Study of Hegemony on the Prairie Plains*. Columbia: University of Missouri Press, 1992.

Sanders Publishing Company. *Farm Buildings*. Chicago: Breeder's Gazette, 1916.

Sapp, David P. *The 1820 Route of the Boone's Lick Trail across Boone County, Missouri*. Columbia: D. Sapp, 2000.

Sauer, Carl Ortwin. *The Geography of the Ozark Highlands of Missouri*. Chicago: University of Chicago Press, 1920.

Schroeder, Adolf E. *Missouri Origins: The Landscape of Home*. Columbia: University of Missouri Extension Division, 1981.

_____. "The Immigrant Experience: Guidelines for Collectors." Columbia: University of Missouri, 1976.

_____. "Preface." In Anna Kemper Hesse (ed.), *Hermann, 1895–1920: A Golden Era of German-American Culture in Missouri* (ms., Hermann, Mo., 1991).

_____, ed. *Concordia, Missouri: A Heritage Preserved*. Columbia: University of Missouri Western Manuscript Collection, 1996.

_____ and Carla Schulz-Geisberg, eds. *Hold Dear, As Always: Jette, A German Immigrant Life in Letters*. Columbia: University of Missouri Press, 1988.

Schroeder, Walter A. *Bibliography of Missouri Geography*. Columbia: University of Missouri Extension Division, 1977.

_____. "Rural Settlement Patterns of the German-Missourian Cultural Landscape." In Marshall and Goodrich (eds.), *The German-American Experience in Missouri* (Columbia 1985), pp. 25–44.

_____. *Opening the Ozarks: A Historical Geography of Missouri's Ste. Genevieve District 1760–1830*. Columbia: University of Missouri Press, 2002.

Schultz, LeRoy G. *Barns, Stables, and Outbuildings: A World Bibliography in English, 1700–1983*. Jefferson N.C.: McFarland, 1986.

Sculle, Keith A. and H. Wayne Price. "The Traditional Barns of Hardin County, Illinois: A Survey and Interpretation." *Material Culture* 25:1 (1993).

_____. "Barns of Nonorthogonal Plan." In A. Noble and H. Wilhelm, *Barns of the Midwest* (1995).

Sears, Roebuck Catalogue. Chicago, Illinois, 1908.

Sheals, Debbie Oakson. "British-American Stonework in Mid-Missouri: A Study in Vernacular Architecture." Thesis, University of Missouri Department of Art History and Archaeology, 1993.

_____. "Cultural Assimilation and Architecture: German Building Traditions in Washington, Missouri." *Missouri Folklore Society Journal* 23 (2001), pp. 17–40.

Shoemaker, Alfred L. *The Pennsylvania Barn*. Kutztown: Pennsylvania Folklife Society, 1959.

Sizemore, Jean. *Ozark Vernacular Houses*. Fayetteville: University of Arkansas Press, 1994.

Skaggs, John Paul. "Rural Life in Madison County: Over 200 Years of Local Agriculture." *Democrat News* (Fredericktown, April 18, 1999).

Sloane, Eric. *A Museum of Early American Tools*. New York: W. Funk, 1964.

_____. *An Age of Barns*. New York: Ballantine Books, 1967.

_____. *American Barns and Covered Bridges*. New York: W. Funk, 1954.

Snider, Becky L. "The Round Barn Form: Functionality, Spiritualism, or Aesthetics?" *Missouri Folklore Society Journal* 22 (2000), pp. 13–26.

Sparks, Laura. "The Burton-Wight House and the Bruns House: Vernacular Architecture and Ethnicity on the Missouri Frontier." Thesis, University of Missouri–Columbia, 1994.

St. Louis County Historic Buildings Commission. *Historic Buildings in St. Louis County*. Clayton, 1985.

Standard Atlas of Randolph County Missouri. Chicago: George A. Ogle Company, 1910.

State Board of Agriculture. *Twenty-Second Annual Report of the State Board of Agriculture for the Years 1889–1890*. Jefferson City: Tribune Publishing Company, 1890.

State Historical Society of Missouri, Comp. *Historic Missouri: A Pictorial Narrative*. Columbia, 1977.

Stewart, Charles A. "The Nail Trade in Missouri: Archaeological Evidence at the Hickman House." *Missouri Folklore Society Journal* 22 (2000), pp. 1–12.

Stipe, Robert E., ed. *New Directions in Rural Preservation*. Washington: U.S. Department of Interior, HCRS, 1980.

Stryker, Roy Emerson and Nancy Wood. *In This Proud Land: America 1935–1943 as Seen in the FSA Photographs*. Boston: New York Graphic Society, 1973.

Summers, Joseph S. and Dottie S. Dallmeyer. *Jefferson City, Missouri*. Chicago: Arcadia Press, 2000.

Thurman, Melvin D. *Building a House in 18th Century Ste. Genevieve*. Ste. Genevieve, Mo.: Pendragon's Press, 1984.

Tishler, William H. "Survey and Inventory Procedures for Historic and Cultural Features in Rural Areas." *Echoes of History* 6 (October 1976), pp. 54–57.

_____. "The Site Arrangement of Rural Farmsteads." *APT Bulletin* 10:1 (1978), pp. 63–78.

Tobacco Institute. *Missouri and Tobacco: A Chapter in America's Industrial Growth*. Washington: Tobacco Institute, 1960).

Upton, Dell, ed. *America's Architectural Roots: Ethnic Groups that Built America*. Washington: National Trust for Historic Preservation, 1986.

_____ and John Michael Vlach, eds. *Common Places: Readings in American Vernacular Architecture*. Athens: University of Georgia Press, 1986.

Van Ravenswaay, Charles, ed. *WPA Guide to 1930s Missouri*. Federal Writers Project 1941. Reprint, St. Louis: Missouri Historical Society, 1998.

_____, ed. "Architecture of the Boon's Lick Country." *Bulletin of the Missouri Historical Society* 6:4 (July 1950), pp. 491–502.

_____. *The Arts and Architecture of German Settlements in Missouri: Survey of a Vanishing Culture*. Columbia: University of Missouri Press, 1977.

Vlach, John Michael. *Barns*. New York: W. W. Norton, 2003.

Waller, Alexander H. *History of Randolph County, Missouri*. Cleveland and Topeka: Historical Publishing Co., 1920.

Walls, Robert, et al., eds. *The Old Traditional Way of Life: Essays in Honor of Warren E. Roberts*. Bloomington, Ind.: Trickster Press, 1989.

Watson, Carrie J. "A Remnant of the Booneslick Trail." *Missouri Folklore Society Journal* 23 (2001), pp. 1–16.

Wells, Wilson L. *Barns in the U.S.A.* Escondido, Calif.: Acme Printing Company, 1976.

Weslager, C. W. *The Log Cabin in America*. New Brunswick, N.J.: Rutgers University Press, 1969.

Williams, Walter. *The State of Missouri: An Autobiography*. Columbia: E. W. Stephens, 1904.

_____, ed. *A History of Northeast Missouri*. Chicago: Lewis Publishing Company, 1913.

Windell, Marie George, ed. "Westward along the Boone's Lick Trail in 1826. The Diary of Colonel John Glover." *Missouri Historical Review* 39:2 (January 1945), pp. 184–199.

Withers, Robert Steele. "The Stake and Rider Fence." *Missouri Historical Review* 44:3 (April 1950), pp. 225–231.

Wood, W. Raymond and R. Bruce McMillan, eds. *Prehistoric Man and His Environments: A Case Study in the Ozark Highlands*. New York: Academic Press, 1976.

Woodforde, J. *Farm Buildings*. London: Routledge and Kegan Paul, 1983.

Wood-Jones, Raymond B. *Traditional Domestic Architecture of the Banbury Region*. Manchester, England: Manchester University Press, 1963.

Wyckoff, Don G. and Jack L. Hoffman, eds. *Pathways to Plains Prehistory*. Oklahoma Anthropological Society Memoir 3 (1982).

Wysocky, Ken, ed. *This Old Barn*. Greendale, Wisc.: Reiman Publications, 1996.

Timber frame barn in Adair County. (Pat B. Clark)

Timber frame barn southwest of Kirksville, Adair County. (Pat B. Clark)

Barn in Randolph County, formerly on Highway 63, south of Jacksonville. (Pat B. Clark)

INDEX

ABOUT THE AUTHOR

Howard Wight Marshall is Professor Emeritus of Art History and Archaeology at the University of Missouri–Columbia, where he was department chair and director of the Missouri Cultural Heritage Center. A Marine Corps veteran, Marshall took his B.A. in English at Missouri and his Ph.D. in Folklore at Indiana University. Marshall taught vernacular architecture, traditional arts, and historic preservation and

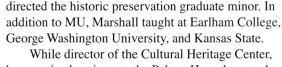

directed the historic preservation graduate minor. In addition to MU, Marshall taught at Earlham College, George Washington University, and Kansas State.

While director of the Cultural Heritage Center, he organized projects at the Pelster Housebarn and University research farms. His articles on the Pelster Housebarn and the Cornett Farm, as well as articles on white-oak basket making in Missouri and town planning in frontier Nevada, are used in college courses. Marshall's projects at MU included recording farm buildings in the lowlands of Scotland as Research Fellow in the European Ethnological Research Centre in the National Museum of Scottish Antiquities.

Previously, Marshall directed research at Conner Prairie Pioneer Settlement, an outdoor museum in Indiana. He then worked five years at the American Folklife Center in the Library of Congress in Washington. He led research teams in Virginia, North Carolina, Georgia, Colorado, and Nevada. His Nevada project led to a Smithsonian Institution exhibition ("Buckaroos in Paradise") and a book, *Paradise Valley, Nevada: The People and Buildings of an American Place*.

Marshall has authored numerous articles and books, including *Folk Architecture in Little Dixie: A Regional Culture in Missouri* and *Vernacular Architecture in Rural and Small Town Missouri*. Marshall's current projects include books on historic buildings (with Osmund Overby) and traditional fiddle music in Missouri.

A native of Moberly, Marshall's family came from Virginia, North Carolina, and Kentucky in the 1820s and 1830s. Branches of the family were engaged in farming, coal mining, railroads, law, teaching, banking, and public service. His late mother, Frances Jennings Marshall, was a local historian and writer who inspired her son's interest in the environment, old buildings, and grass-roots history.

Dr. Marshall and his wife, Margot Ford McMillen, operate a small livestock farm in Callaway County.